BECOMING A BILLIONAIRE LAND BANKER

How I built my multi-billion Real Estate empire from Zero-up

DR. STEPHEN AKINTAYO

Copyright © 2023 Dr. Stephen Akintayo

ISBN: 9798378433667

All rights reserved. No part of this publication may be reproduced, distributed, or transmitted in any form or by any means, including photocopying, recording, or other electronic or mechanical methods, without the prior written permission of the publisher, except in the case of brief quotations embodied in critical reviews and certain other noncommercial uses permitted by copyright law.

For permission requests, write to the publisher, addressed "Attention: Permissions Coordinator," at the address below;

POX 888442,
Burj Khalifa,
Dubai, UAE.
info@stephenakintayo.com
www.stephenakintayo.com
+971588283572.
+2348180000618.

DISCLAIMER

This book is not intended for use as a source of legal, business, accounting or financial advice.

All readers are advised to seek the services of competent professionals in legal, business, accounting and finance fields. While reasonable attempts have been made to ensure the accuracy of the information provided in this publication, the author does not assume any responsibility for errors, omissions or contrary interpretations of this information and any damages or costs incurred by that. While examples of past results may be used occasionally in this work, they are intended to be for purposes of example only.

The contents of this book are based solely on the personal experiences and proven track record of success of the author. The author does not assume any responsibility or liability whatsoever for what you choose to do with this information. Use your judgement. Any perceived slight of specific people or organisations, and any resemblance to characters living, dead or otherwise, real or fictitious, is purely unintentional. You are encouraged to print this book for easy reading. However, you use this information at your own risk.

IMPORTANT LEGAL INFORMATION

This book is © Dr. Stephen Akintayo. All Rights Reserved. You may not sell this book, give it away, display it publicly, or may you distribute it in any form whatsoever.

While reasonable attempts have been made to ensure the accuracy of the information provided in this publication, the author does not assume any responsibility for errors, omissions, or contrary interpretations of this information and any damages or costs incurred by that.

This book is not intended for use as a source of legal, business, accounting, or financial advice. All readers are advised to seek the services of competent professionals in the legal, business, accounting, and finance fields. While examples of past results may be used occasionally in this work, they are intended to be for purposes of example only.

No representation is made or implied that the reader will do as well by using any of the techniques mentioned in this book. The contents of this book are based solely on the personal experiences of the author. The author does not assume any responsibility or liability whatsoever for what you choose to do with this information. Use your judgement.

Any perceived slight of specific people or organisations, and any resemblance to characters living, dead or otherwise, real or fictitious, is purely unintentional. You are encouraged to print this book for easy reading. However, you use this information at your own risk.

DEDICATION

To my Mother, who was the first person to open my eyes to land banking;

To my father, who taught me about the real estate business;

To every individual who seeks to build wealth legitimately through land banking.

ACKNOWLEDGEMENT

My utmost gratitude goes to God Almighty, the maker of men, for He has made me out of nothing.

I want to thank Mr Niyi Adeleye, who helped me begin my land banking journey by giving me 50 acres of land to sell based on trust. Thank you for trusting me to deliver, sir.

Thanks to my family for their contributions and support, especially to my lovely wife and my understanding children.

I gratefully acknowledge the recognition and support of my spiritual and business mentors.

To all members of staff of Gtext Holdings for their feedback and unending support and encouragement, I appreciate you all.

I also appreciate my team at Stephen Akintayo Consulting for working tirelessly to put this work together.

I love you all!

CONTENTS

Title Page
Copyright
Disclaimer
Important Legal Information
Dedication
Acknowledgement
Introduction

PART ONE	1
CHAPTER 1	2
CHAPTER 2	5
CHAPTER 3	13
CHAPTER 4	20
CHAPTER 5	29
CHAPTER 6	46
PART TWO	55
CHAPTER 7	56
CHAPTER 8	71
PART THREE	78
CHAPTER 9	79
CHAPTER 10	84
PART FOUR	94
CHAPTER 11	95
CHAPTER 12	103
CHAPTER 13	117

CHAPTER 14	121
PART FIVE	127
CHAPTER 15	128
CHAPTER 16	131
CHAPTER 17	135
CHAPTER 18	142
PART SIX	151
CHAPTER 19	152
CHAPTER 20	154
GTEXT HOMES PROPERTIES AND LOCATIONS	157
About The Author	171
OTHER BOOKS BY THE SAME AUTHOR	179
GTEXT HOMES OFFICES AROUND THE WORLD	183
CONNECT WITH DR. STEPHEN AKINTAYO ON THESE SOCIAL MEDIA PLATFORMS	185

INTRODUCTION

REAL ESTATE IS MY WINNING TICKET!

As you go through the pages of this book, you will understand why I said so and why I have so dearly taken up the gospel of Real Estate.

Often, people doubt the genuineness of my wealth. They are in constant awe of how a boy from a poverty-stricken background could be this successful.

Well, land banking is the absolute goldmine that gives you genuine wealth.

You know, I remember when I got to the house my mother built in Lagos, I was disappointed. I asked myself, "Why would my mother build a house in this location?"

Then I didn't have much knowledge of houses and lands. I knew nothing about Real Estate. But years later, I understood that my mother had foresight. She knew we would need that house one day. Today that land she bought for N8,000 is worth millions of naira.

One thing about land is that it's not about the location but the tendency for it to appreciate as time goes on. Unfortunately, most people are still procrastinating when investing in landed properties. One thing is sure, if you fail to invest today, you will pay those who did a higher percentage.

In this book, I have expatriated all you need to know to build wealth through land banking. From acquiring land to finding the right source, a good location, the perfect land size, documentation and developmental levies, identifying land fraud, calculating the returns on investment, the process of reselling your land etc., have all been treated in this book.

This book entails practical measures I have used in building a profitable multi-billion Real Estate empire from Zero up and how you can replicate the same.

Remember, you are not a rich man until you own land. It's an asset that keeps you appreciating and helps you build wealth over time.

I desire that after reading this book; you'll make a conscious decision to invest in land banking and start building wealth for yourself and your generations.

I love you,
Dr Stephen Akintayo.

PART ONE
KNOWLEDGE ACQUISITION ENTITY IN REAL ESTATE

CHAPTER 1
Introduction to Land Banking

Land banking is the process of land aggregation or buying of fortunes of land for development or investment, meaning you are buying the land so that in future, you're able to sell it at a higher price and get good returns

FACTORS TO CONSIDER IN LAND BANKING

1. POPULATION GROWTH

I tell people that the primary reason one should invest in Nigeria is population growth. Data has shown that Africa is still the one that keeps rising in terms of population growth. Once there's population growth, the land will never decrease, and because of the vast population growth, there will always be a need for shelter.

2. LABOUR

Creating jobs in that vicinity, like Universities, Churches, and all these public facilities drives the value of land banking and real estate in specific locations. You also look at factors like factories and road dualisation. Once certain roads are dualised, more companies want property facing the expressway.

3. CREDIBLE COMPANY

Another major factor is the integrity of those you are buying from, not those who sell to multiple people; ensure that you're buying from a credible company with integrity and a track record, that is, a company that will do it as a proper transaction.

4. MENTORSHIP

Mentorship means having someone who has been in the business, whom you can look up to and who can give you advice, not family members who don't even have a plot of land, so in the process of doing land banking, have people who have done it who have made it, who can mentor and guide you in the investment.

EXAMPLES OF LAND BANKING INVESTORS

Chief Razaq Okoya is a significant industrialist in Lagos and Nigeria, but at some point, industries crashed in Nigeria; what sustained him was the lands he invested in; Eleganza is back now. So when you understand population growth, you achieve a lot in land banking.

Another example is the General Overseer of the Redeemed Christian Church of God, Pastor E.A. Adeboye. Although he had the same vision, the Church moved to Mowe and bought land for Eleven Thousand Naira per plot, but today we know how much a plot of land costs at the Redemption Camp.

HOW TO GROW YOUR INVESTMENT AS A LAND BANKER

START SMALL

I always advise you to start small. My first commercial investment in land banking was a property in Ikorodu. The place was waterlogged, and even the road to get to my land was not there, but I envisaged the prospect and value that the place holds; some of those properties I got for seven hundred and Fifty Thousand Naira per plot. Start with what you have. The properties you acquire over the year appreciate; you can sell and then diversify; it's usually the starting point. The first step is getting the land, and then you go on to secure it before talking about investment, though, unfortunately, in real estate, it takes a while before you start making profits.

For example, Dubai was a desert, but today we all know the value of the place; it took a while for the infrastructure to come alive. Even for someone who does not have money, you can sell for a real estate company and then use your commission from sales to acquire land, resell after some years, and develop others for rent. One important thing to note is that land investments come with many issues, but they can quickly and easily be resolved;

the system is never perfect. In Gtext, we use technology for transparency so that it is easy to engage investors, even those in the diaspora, as the company does immediate allocation and can send documents to investors anywhere in the world. Communication is vital in business; don't wait to buy land; buy land and wait.

Conclusively, Real estate helps you to make and manage money; it helps you to multiply the money that helps you to transfer it to the next generation. Real estate is the only way to transfer wealth to the next generation.

CHAPTER 2
How To Identify The Right Location For Land Banking Investment In Nigeria

About a year ago, I held a Facebook live session from my office in Dubai where I shared *'How to identify the right location in Land banking and Real Estate investment to make millions in profits in Nigeria'*. Many people joined from several countries, including Cameroon, Ghana, Manchester, Nigeria, and more countries. It was a fantastic session, and I will share several of what we discussed in this chapter.

You must have heard how this business started with just a thousand Naira; today, it has grown to become a multi-billion naira corporation. So, I will be sharing a few of the principles I have engaged in the past and at present, which are working wonders in land banking and real estate investment.

This chapter is not a motivational write-up or a theoretical subject I went to learn in class. So please pay attention to get the best because you will gain knowledge from my experiences. So, how do we identify the correct location for land banking and real estate investment in Nigeria? I will share four significant points to identify them as we progress.

Firstly, you must identify the properties close to a densely populated city. In order words, *consider a location close to a significant or mega city or an outskirt of a major city.*

A dense city is a city with a high population of people. Since we are focusing on Nigeria, we can consider places like Lagos and Abuja as highly dense, and internationally, Dubai is a highly populated city.

Why, then, should we consider locations close to these cities? Because people will soon begin to migrate from the highly populated and expensive cities to more affordable places. Of course, humans are naturally wired for pleasure and do not want stress; they prefer quieter and calmer locations. Because of this, the value of the lands on the outskirts of the major cities begins to increase. So, the best places to do land banking in Nigeria are locations close to a major city. That is one of the powerful secrets of land banking.

Currently, Lagos State is a considerable location for land banking in Nigeria. Therefore, you should consider locations like Ibeju-Lekki, Epe, Ota, Atan, Idi Iroko, Gbadagri, Ikorodu, and Lagos-Ibadan Expressway. If you are smart, you should look for these places to do land banking. Why these Locations? Studies have shown that the population of Lagos increases by 50 people every minute, meaning more than 50 people relocate to Lagos every day. People from rural areas relocate to Lagos daily because they feel that's the best place to make it. Even in Nigerian movies shot in the village, we see that everyone wants to move to Lagos to start a new life because there has been this perception that those who live in Lagos are the ones making it. Even Goldman Sachs confirmed that the best location to purchase a property in Africa to get the highest return on investment is Lagos, the second location is Abuja, and the third is Port Harcourt. Also, Johannesburg and one other South African city and the rest follow, so Lagos is a big-time mega city.

Another great fact is this; the most expensive land in the world is also in Lagos, and it's not even Eko Atlantic at the moment; it is Banana Island.

Let me share one shocking thing about Banana Island; per square metre of land in Banana Island is within the range of 650 million - 900 million naira. In case you don't know what a square metre is, a square metre is a unit of area equal to a square, one metre on each side. Yes, it's funny and crazy, and it doesn't make sense, but that's the fact. You would have said New York, but New York has the most expensive properties and sky air rights worldwide because they don't sell land anymore; they now sell floors.

Currently, the ground owners wouldn't give it up in Manhattan, so people purchase floors instead of land. Developers (Land bankers) in Manhattan do not buy the ground anymore, so usually, they go check out for floors. For instance, maybe it's a 30-story building, so they then negotiate with the owner on rebuilding his entire building, and when they do, they will increase it to 70 floors; I'll give you back your 30 floors, I will take 40 floors, and I'll still pay you for the project.

That is a true story; there is a guy who is a big-time billionaire developer in Manhattan today. It is not Donald Trump, but he's a new person. He's been doing big stuff, so he has one of the largest Malls in Manhattan. He saw a property opposite him, and he did everything to purchase it from the owner, but the owner refused to sell it, So he thought of what to do to get the land; then he paid the owner 250 million dollars, took over the property and rebuilt it. Of course, the owner returned his floors to where they were before, and the developer kept the ones above. It's crazy about New York Manhattan; you should study Manhattan to understand real estate globally.

Finally, on this point, I have always said that Africans don't teach what they know; they hoard information, which is why many Africans are poor. When you know something that will help you become rich, and you do not share it with others, they cannot know, which is why people are poor in Africa. Sadly, what Africans spread about is gossip - who had a sex rape, who slept with whose wife, things that would not add any value to either party is what we discuss even on the radio, television and social media. We waste so much time and energy discussing things that add no value to us.

Secondly, invest in a property close to a new government or industrial project area, like a free trade zone.

If you're buying a property close to a free trade zone, you are hitting gold because companies will move to that area soon. On the other hand, if you purchase a property close to a refinery or a major industrial project, it shows you are smart about land banking because you are making the right decisions. Suppose you are also buying close to a significant university area. In that case, you're making the best decision - because lecturers of that university would buy properties around where the university is so they can have easy access to their workplaces. *So, the second central point is buying a property close to a new project, such as a university area, a government project area, a free trade zone, a refinery, or an industrial complex.*

Someone would ask me, but Dr Stephen, if I buy a property close to a refinery, what about the fact that there will be traffic because of companies in that area? Listen carefully; I am not saying you are buying the property to live in it. The point I am driving at is that - you should buy it to sell in future.

So, when doing land banking, you are not thinking of living in the property you purchased; you are investing for the future. So when thinking of land banking, you are thinking of investments but not building your family home. As I said, consider investment first for a profit before buying a property for personal shelter.

Some would say, I cannot live on the Island, so I cannot buy land there. Nobody is asking you to live there; think wisely. You do not need to live there; buy it to sell it in the future. I do not live on the Island, but I own four estates there. Some people want to live on the Island, which matters. So I buy properties to make a profit from them.

When you're doing land banking, do not purchase properties in the locations you love alone; purchase where customers prefer and invest in areas where the population is migrating - and places where the population is increasing rapidly. Again, it's about people and customers.

You can also consider somewhere close to the airport. It does not matter if the location is in a bush. For example, our new Asaba Estate is about 15 minutes drive from the airport. That's why we got it, and it is on the express. We built a massive estate there just because it is close to the airport. These are secrets I am sharing with you.

In the 60s and 70s, nobody liked Ikeja; it was bush, and that is why the government established an airport there. But, of course, an airport is not situated close to the city because of the movement, but guess what? The smart ones invested in Ikeja years ago, and today, they are rich and multi-billionaires because they did land banking smartly.

Some of the people who invested in Ikeja were not living there, but because they understood land banking, they understood the profits in land banking; they got those properties and tied them down for years and later flipped them. So they got colossal money in return, and today, their children are grateful. Some did not sell it during their lifetime, so they passed it on to their children as an inheritance. Their children sold the properties for a considerable amount of money, and they are making a whole lot of money from it.

As I said, get properties close to new projects, but let me place a warning, do not do land banking close to your village or in your village; you will not make any profit from it.

Someone reached out to me recently and asked when I was going to visit Akure, so I asked what was happening in Akure. I do not have a plot of land in my village, but I would still build a massive mansion, so don't get me wrong. But first, I need to make enough money in locations with enormous profits, after which I can think of what I can do for my village. I may decide to build a big mansion or start a big farm because I intend to give back to my village, and two poor people cannot help themselves, so I have to make it elsewhere before going to establish something in my village. In summary, make money before returning to your village to do something. That is what intelligent people do.

Yes, lands are now expensive in Akure, but that's not the point. Usually, I would make more money in Lagos, Abuja, Port Harcourt, and Asaba than in Akure so that I would build those locations first. You would even make more money in Ibadan and Abeokuta compared to Akure. It doesn't mean that Akure is not growing; you need to understand the indices of land banking.

Do not do land banking with emotions. So many Africans will build houses in their villages where nobody will bid for it, and in years to come, because nobody lives in it, the building begins to develop cracks, and the entire property turns out to be a mess; what a wasteful way of investing.

I say a lot that one of the reasons Africans are poor is because we are wasteful. You hear about someone who went to build a property with 2 Billion Naira to impress people. Instead, you could build a massive estate with that money and make huge profits.

There is nothing wrong with spending 2 Billion Naira in building a property, but when you have yet to arrive, it is not wise to rush things. Take your time, and build yourself. When you haven't arrived, and you start showing off to your village people, this is where many people meet their death. Because you haven't arrived, you start going to show off in the village, and before you know it, you will say the witches of the village have finished your career.

I tell people this: make sure you've made enough money that even if the witches come to your business, they will eat it and die there. One Yoruba adage says; if your hand has not touched the cutlass, do not ask what killed your father. So there is a phase in your life where you need to build your wealth in places where you get good returns before returning to your village to show off.

So, do not do land banking in the village. You can give back to the village, but do not invest there because you will not get returns. The property may not appreciate ten years from now, so know that for a fact.

Thirdly, identify locations with good town planning. One of the best ways to do land banking is to invest in locations with good town planning. You may have to ask what the project plans for that location are. When I want to do land banking, I always look for a well-planned estate. Though they may not have the money to work out their plans yet, be sure they have a well-structured plan.

I remember my uncle, the first principal of Ojodu Grammar School, Lagos, in the 90s. He shared the history of Omole, Berger and Magodo in Lagos. He was privileged to know those things because he was the first principal of Ojodu Grammar School. He also lived in that area and was involved in selling many properties in the same place. He told me the history of how many of these locations were thick forests. He was faced with assassination attempts three times. That is how thick a forest Berger, Lagos was. Then, the closest police station was in Alausa.

He shared with me about one of the assassination attempts, how he woke up in the morning and had to go in a pool of blood to report to the station about the assassination attempt on him.

In those days, they started planning Omole Phase 1 and Magodo, including places with marshy lands and others with dry land. At that time, they always said they had a plan, but there was nothing to prove it, but some people believed it and invested in it, and today they are smiling at profits. I bought a property in Magodo from one of my friends; knowing how much he bought and sold it to me, the difference is enormous.

So, with good town planning, you are sure of an excellent investment. You may need to pay more than any other place, but it's a good move because it will be worth it.

Finally, get a mentor. There are two aspects of life that you must not go through without a mentor, and they are; Marriage and Money. These are two significant areas you do not learn in school. For marriage, you are given a certificate before starting the journey. So under money, we have land and buying land from someone is almost like a lifetime marriage. Secondly, the money involved is heavy, so do not do it without getting a mentor. Only go into buying properties when you already have a proper understanding of them. It doesn't matter if you need to pay for it.

I shared with you about one of my students who bought a property in Nicon Estate about eighteen years ago. Two years ago, we sold the property for 220 Million Naira. He paid 12 million for that property; fifteen years later, he sold it for 220 Million Naira. Did he lose if he paid 1 million naira to get someone to mentor him in buying that property in Nicon Estate? Of course, he didn't because he sold the property for 220 million naira fifteen years later. Even considering inflation, that is a crazy profit. Let's say inflation every year for 15 years was 16%; that is still a crazy profit. A property you bought for 12 million naira is now selling for 220 million naira. That's the kind of money we are talking about in land banking. And this happens all over the world.

Here in Dubai, we sold a property to a company called Shoba. The owner purchased the properties for as low as 20,000 dirhams, 50,000 dirhams, and 100,000 dirhams, respectively. Now, such an area of land is sold for 10 million dirhams. So get a mentor!

Finally, one of the ways to maximise land banking is to add value to the land you bought. In a few chapters from here, I will share how to add value to your land.

I hope you have learnt something; see you in the next chapter.

CHAPTER 3
Knowing Land Fraud And Why Lagos State Has Most Of It

Recently, a seemingly ordinary act among folks purchasing challenging land properties has come to my attention. Many people do not know what to look out for when acquiring landed properties, leading to them being a victim of nemesis.

In this chapter, I'll share what to notice when buying a property to ensure you're safe and protected against being defrauded, cheated, or scammed.

How Do You Recognise Land Fraud?

1. When the Land is Cheap

Particularly in Lagos, gone are the days of cheap land purchases. Thus, if anyone tells you to come to buy land in Lagos at a certain ridiculous lower amount, flee! Do you know why? That's pure deception. Any land with C of O offered to you by a real estate company for less than ten million naira should be rechecked. Something is likely off. The reason is that all the charges involved in processing the C of O alone cannot be less than 3 million naira. So, would the land owner give you the land for free or at his loss? We are often victims of not being aware and not having the proper knowledge. **Whenever the land is cheap, something is not correct.**

People in the diaspora are often the victims of such. That is because they are often ignorant of the prices of landed properties. Some believe that properties are supposed to be cheap; they believe anyone selling higher is trying to defraud them. In many cases, that notion is not valid. For Your Information (FYI), Lagos State has the most expensive land in the world.

Eko Atlantic used to be a sand-filled bar beach. That project is one of the projects they believe would change Lagos. It is over one million square metres and is one of the most expensive locations. Almost every part of Lagos was sand-filled, including Banana Island. The population of land is minimal. Whenever I hear people talk about dry lands in Lagos, I am tickled with laughter. It's almost nonexistent; virtually every dry place today was sand-filled. They are trying to get more land, that is why it is expensive. Banana Island is the most expensive land in the world. It's over one million dollars to get 600 square metres in Banana Island. There's no more land; they're just sand-filling the lagoon to get more land, and the cost of sand-filling is high. Specifically, the land is majorly purchased by high-profile people. That's why the most expensive land is in Lagos State. It could have been New York, but they don't have any more land in Manhattan.

So, stop looking for cheap land in Lagos, as it just doesn't exist! People can deceive you into it, and it's one of the most significant ways they scam people. Now, you know better than to fall for such.

Anytime someone proposes land sales to you in Lagos at an unbelievable price, always ask, "Why is this land this cheap?" A land with C of O in Lagos cannot be less than 10 Million Naira, except if it has no documents. *So if it is cheap, it is a red flag.*

Title and location always determine the price of a landed property. **Gazette** can still be obtained between 7 and 8 Million Naira, but not lower. If it's cheaper than that, something is wrong.

I met a woman in Dubai some years ago; she was saying she wanted to purchase land in Ajah, Lagos State. I asked her the reason behind such a decision, and she stated her intention to own a warehouse with much attention paid to proximity. She further mentioned how she desires land free from government acquisition. I asked for her budget, and she replied that her budget was 8 million naira. I frankly told her, "Ma, you cannot get land in Ajah for 8 million naira free from government acquisition." That was about five years ago. So, it's a lot more expensive than five years ago. I told her I could get her one of 6 million naira in Ibeju-Lekki that even had a C of O. She insisted on getting Ajah and called another company, and they deceived her that it wasn't under acquisition, though it had no C of O. She was about to start work when she discovered the land was a road.

There are types of government acquisitions. For some, the government would still release the land, but for a case such as a road construction, you just have to let it go. The express road was supposed to pass that land. How on earth could she get such land? That was how she was swindled out of 8 million naira.

Sometimes, I have bought and sold the land under acquisition; it was a risk, but not land that was clearly stated for road construction. Unfortunately, there's no way to approach the government and ask them to give you back the land.

Many people are victims of this because they want a particular location, but they want it cheap. I tell people that we have to learn to overcome greed. Anytime we are victims of scams, it's always a function of greed. You have to be greedy for someone to be able to scam you. You may not know, but if you're looking for something less than the actual value, that's greed. Every time people get scammed, some people take advantage of their greed.

I have never been scammed online. Before I buy anything, I must be sure of the actual value of that thing. I make enquiries. So, when you're giving me a specific price that is way lower than the actual value, I know there's something, and I would ask questions, and you'd be surprised that I'm asking why it's cheap since people do not usually ask that kind of question, instead, they say it's too expensive and that the price should be reduced.

In buying a landed property, I would always research how much the land is, the cheap and the expensive.

2. A Developed Location Sold At Ridiculous "Awoof" Prices

When a location is developed and still cheap, that is a red flag. Why is it cheap despite being developed? For example, if you want to buy land in Ikeja GRA and you're asked to pay 50 million naira for 600 square metres, you should ask them why. Something is not adding up. Regularly, the price of land in Ikeja GRA ranges from 100 to 200 million naira. In Ogba, you can get land worth 30-35 million naira, but not Ikeja GRA. When a location is developed, and they want to sell the land cheaply, you should make enquiries. It doesn't mean it's impossible, but you should ask questions at least. If the owner needs money urgently due to health reasons, it's understandable, yet, I would still want to investigate, even with medical reports to be sure the person is sick and needs money for treatment.

I know of a case like that, where the landowner took a bank loan and died. His wife didn't know he owed a bank, and when the lawyer got involved, she was asked to sell the land and give the bank their money back. In the mind of these, the seller doesn't mind how much they are selling the property; they want the court case to end. In that case, it's up to me whether I want to take that risk. But in a location that is already developed and the property is ridiculously cheap, that is suspicious. It would be best if you were careful about properties like this.

3. When Ọmọ Onilẹ̀ (Indigenes) Are The Ones Selling The Land To You

When you buy from the indigenous people, you should be worried about not whether the land belongs to them; instead, you should be worried about the position you are on the list of buyers of that same land. Are you the tenth, fifth or twentieth? They often sell the same land to at least 5-10 people.

Buying land from **Ọmọ Onilẹ** is one of the most dangerous things you can do because they often sell the same land to several persons who end up fighting over the same land, and the person with the biggest muscles win. I'm sure you don't want that. Sometimes, it gets diabolical and messy.

On the other hand, real estate agencies can survive because they buy in bulk. They can afford to do all the P.R. and care for the families during all the festive seasons. Sometimes, they can even buy the king of the land a car. How would one who bought just one plot be able to afford that? There's a lot that real estate companies do to keep the interest of their investors that you may not be able to do as an individual who decided to buy land directly from the indigenous people. I always advise buying land from real estate companies and not directly from indigenes. If you disagree with real estate companies, you can have intelligent conversations or even sue them in court. If it were to be indigenes, it might not be so. If you deal with one person, he can disappear. It is better to look for credible companies and buy from them.

4. Only Buy From Real Estate Companies That Have Structure

Structures include a website and an office; if you type their name on google business, it must show where their office is located. They must have a structure outside the owners. One of the biggest mistakes I've seen in Africa is people trying to do business with just one man. Stop buying from a one-person business. It is essential to know the company's owners, but it shouldn't be one man; there must be a structure. They must have an office, and there must be people who can attend to me. I should be able to email the company and talk to them so that they can address my concerns.

You don't want to do a one-person business; the owner can die. You want to buy from companies with structure. Anyone that knows what I'm teaching cannot fall victim to scams. People wouldn't have lost their money if they knew these things. Many buy based on the fact that they knew the seller personally, perhaps their uncle, cousin and others, or because they've seen the land. It's not about seeing the land, I would instead buy from a company that I've never seen the land and I've never been to, but I've gone online and seen that they have a structure (a website, an office) rather than someone showing me the land. The land may not be there tomorrow; they can sell it to someone else. If it's a company with structure, I can sue them and get my money back. We must get this part.

5. When You See Companies That Owners Are Unknown, You Are About To Be Defrauded

This doesn't mean the owner must work in the company, as I'm withdrawing gradually from our company's day-to-day running, but the owner has to be known. Several people in this country, kings and retired military personnel, have companies and are not involved in the business's day-to-day activities, but they are known as the owner, and they are not ashamed to be associated with the company.

When you can't know the company's owner and go ahead to buy properties from them, you are not safe. You may see adverts in the media, but who is the owner? Are they people of repute? Are they people who can't run away because they have a brand to protect? Are they people who would want their brand to deliver consistently?

These are very critical issues that we often don't look at. You often just come to Nigeria to see the land and return. That doesn't matter. They can package the land for you to see, and you're on your own when you return. Be careful of companies without anyone associated with them; you might be scammed or defrauded. Always ask the questions, "Who are the owners? Who is the face of the company?"

Gtext Homes is a company of which I am the Managing Director. Not only is my face seen with the brand, but also other faces ranging from Jim Iyke to Mercy Aigbe in times past, to Ini Edo, Obesere, Kola Olootu, William Uchemba, Mr Macaroni, Seyi Law, Woli Arole, Woli Agba, Pretty Mike, AY Makun, Official Lolo, Kate Henshaw, Chief Ebenezer Obey and many others. Several reputable people have put their names behind the brand we run. There have to be people. These people not only put their names on the brand but also do adverts on CNN.

These are the things you look out for. Once you see this thing, relax and do business with them. You're always afraid because you don't even know what to look out for. When people don't know what to look out for, they lose big time on their investments. These practical things have made many lose a lot due to ignorance.

CHAPTER 4
Defraud Prevention: Understanding Land Size and Land Documents

I have heard stories of people defrauded regarding property issues, and it's likely that many of us do not understand what property documents or sizes are. Thus, we fall victim often.

I want to start by helping you to understand the various sizes of land that exist. First, it is important to note that in our region, Nigeria, to be precise, the measurement for land is called square metre (sqm), while in places like Dubai, square foot (sqft) is used.

A square foot in Dubai is smaller than a square metre in Nigeria; one square foot equals one metre, while 10.7 square feet is equivalent to one metre. This is the smallest land measurement.

Now that we understand the most diminutive form of measurement in land banking, the next question will be, how many square metres equals one plot?

Generally speaking, things and times change depending on the country you are in and even the property company you're dealing with. Thus, 600 sqm usually equals one plot in Nigeria, particularly Lagos. In Abuja, around 500 sqm equals one plot; often, you either have 540 sqm or 648 sqm, that is, 18 metres by 36 metres giving you 648 sqm, usually the measurement for a standard plot.

It is imperative to ask questions when you're doing property, always ask the company you're buying from to give the size of their plots.

At Gtext Homes, in Lagos, we do 600 square metres, which equals one plot. In Abuja, we do 500 square metres, which is essential to understand. If you don't, you will most likely feel cheated or swindled because you are ignorant of exactly what you are doing.

The next question is, how many plots make one acre? Whatever your measurement of plots, six units of it make one acre. However, typically one acre is about four thousand and forty-six thousand square metres which is the average size of an acre.

The following essential basics you should know in land banking are the number of acres that makes a hectare and how many square metres make a hectare. Approximately 2.4 acres while 10,000 square metres make a hectare.

Most times, ignorance makes people claim they were swindled in the course of the property business because they were not educated and did not do research and were not aware of what they were buying, whereas, in reality, they should have investigated before buying.

TYPES OF LAND

That is also another complex aspect of land banking people struggle to understand.

1. Committed Acquisition

The land with committed acquisition means the government has designated that parcel for a specific project; as such, those parcels of land can never be released to individuals or organisations for development projects.

In Nigeria, you have committed acquisition, while in the U.S. and U.K., you have zoning, where certain lands have been zoned for specific purposes and cannot be used for any other. However, in Nigeria, we have something called acquisition, where the Land Use Decree of 1978, now known as the Land Use Act of 1978, empowers the Governor of a State to be the owner of the land on behalf of the people to build public facilities like hospital, roads and schools.

Now we have situations whereby families have taken the

government to court, and they won the case because they were able to prove that the reason the government took over their land was not for public use, and they were able to get back their property.

So once a land is under committed acquisition, I advise you to run away from that land, for the fact that a piece of land is not in use for its primary purpose does not mean it will be left fallow.

For example, they will sell to you a location where an express road or a bridge is supposed to pass; even if it takes 50 years, that bridge will still be built because as the population grows, the need for the road becomes expedient; imagine the pain the property owner will go through, avoid buying land under committed acquisition.

2. Non-Committed Acquisition

These types of lands fall within government acquisition; however, they are not committed. That means that the government does not have that land earmarked for a particular purpose; this kind of land can be purchased, but the buyer must proceed to ratify its title with the government.

In this situation, because of specific development, the land will be put under acquisition; however, with no specific project earmarked for that area, usually, such land can be reclaimed.

The ratification process after the purchase of a non-committed acquisition of land demands that you take the receipt of purchase to the ministry of lands, pay tax on the land, and you will be issued a temporary permit to build on it over time you complete the ratification (approval, confirmation or authorisation) process so you still have your land intact but note that this can only happen for lands that are not under committed acquisition.

So usually, the government can place acquisition on areas beyond what they immediately have a specific need for.

HOW TO KNOW A LAND UNDER COMMITTED ACQUISITION

a) Take the coordinates of the land and give it to a trusted Surveyor, not to family members. I remember a particular land we were buying in Abuja. I gave this land to somebody to get a surveyor, and the surveyor gave a go-ahead that all documents were genuine, but I later discovered that the C of O was fake. Unfortunately, some surveyors and lawyers do not know their job.

b) Deal with a company with a reputation: Make sure the company you buy from is more significant than the property you are buying. Do business with a credible organisation you can rely on. There are a lot of hidden insights about property deals, particularly in Africa, that you can't figure all out by yourself; get a credible institution that, even if they make a mistake, is going to take responsibility for it.

Another quick example, we purchased this particular property, and the gazette presented to us looked legitimate, even confirmed by a surveyor. Note that these people have insiders in the Ministry of Land that manipulate documents, but when you have some credible people, it will be easy to detect.

I remember telling the investors that the property was under acquisition, and I did my investigation and discovered the area under non-committed acquisition, and work had begun there; all left was the ratification process. So, that's the essence of dealing with a legitimate organisation.

If you have land under committed acquisition, don't go near it, no matter what they say, but a non-committed acquisition of land is a risk you can take.

3. Free land

This land doesn't have any title but is not under any

commitment. It's not committed in any way but doesn't necessarily have a title; this is good land to buy but know that ultimately you still need to do your Certificate of Occupancy.

Now know this, the more perfect the title of the land, the more expensive the land is because this is where many people get scammed. For example, you will see two lands beside each other at Ibeju-Lekki, one selling for N10 million and the other for N2.5 million; what you do not often understand is that the land beside the other one may have a better title.

Anything of value comes with a price; nothing of value is cheap, so when you say that a property is expensive, know that the confidence of someone to charge you is proof that they are ready to offer you value. On the other hand, there is no way someone wants to offer you value and he will give it to you cheaply.

Let me quickly give you two examples; someone told me about a property with a Certificate of Occupancy with a budget of 2.5 million naira, I told him I had an estate in that area and that the whole of that place was under acquisition. The budget was too low to get a place there, but he argued and I on the other hand already had plans to ratify my estate which is also under acquisition in the area, but he was adamant. A few years later, he came back crying.

You will agree that it takes some greed to be scammed; people leverage your desire for a significant discount to scam you of your hard-earned money.

Also, a woman in Dubai told me she wanted to land at Ajah for a warehouse, and her budget was N8 million for two plots. I told her I had a place at Ibeju-Lekki; she said it was too far and that she wanted Ajah. I told her there was no way she would get a plot of land for 4 million naira in Ajah, but she returned and told me she got a place on the express. Two years down the line, she came back lamenting that it was the express road that was sold to her.

When it comes to property, please don't be greedy in buying

property. You must make sure you buy it right, and I can assure you that you will always make money in real estate. Now, let us look at the steps to take when you purchase free land.

What to do when you purchase free land

Do a Provincial Survey: This is a map of the location. With this, you can go to the Ministry of land and process your Certificate of Occupancy (C of O). It ultimately means that the land belongs to you for 99 years. Once the free land is not on the express road or near the express route you are good to go. It might be better to buy land free of any acquisition over time; you can sort out getting the C of O. Sometimes, you realise that the cost of doing that is not as much as when you buy land that's already perfected.

4. An Excised or Gazetted Land

This is the process whereby the government releases a parcel of land back to the indigenous owners of an area for residential and commercial developments. So when the Governor of a State places acquisition on land and later decides to release the land back to the people, then that is excise land. Another type of land is called Allocated Land, where you get a Letter of Allocation. It also happens in places that have been committed. So where they are places that the land has been committed, when the government decides to sell the land, they issue a Letter of Allocation,

However, the perfect one is the Gazetted Land. Publications are usually made on the pages of Newspapers to inform the public about the government's decision to release the land to the people. For excised land, it is released, but no publications are made.

5. Land with C of O

This means land with a Certificate of Occupancy. In Abuja, they give R of O, meaning Right of Occupancy. The Certificate of Occupancy is higher than the Right of Occupancy. You can always go ahead to get a C of O in Abuja, but they mean the same thing: they give you the right to occupy and work on the land.

A Gazetted Land is more powerful than land with a Certificate of Occupancy because a gazette does not expire, but a C of O is for 99 years. A gazette is by the law of proclamation, and you rarely hear that it was revoked, but they often revoke C of O, and a land with a gazette does not need renewal.

6. Land with Governor's Consent

Land with the Governor's consent is land with a global C of O. often, it is not given to an individual; it is given to a more significant number of land. A global C of O means that one person does not own this C of O, and a gazette is usually also given to a village. If you bought the land when it was free to hold, you could decide to go and personally process your land with the government.

LAND DOCUMENTS

To process your Certificate of Occupancy (C of O), you must first survey the land. A survey is a map and measurement of the land you have purchased. It would be best if you got your survey because, without it, you cannot get a Deed of Assignment. The Survey and Deed of Assignment must be in your name.

The Deed of Assignment is the most potent land document in the world, not even the Governor's Consent or C of O because if you do not have a Deed of Assignment in your name, you don't have land, and you cannot build.

The Deed of Assignment transfers ownership from the seller to the buyer, but the C of O and the Governor's Consent does not transfer ownership. Therefore, a Governor's consent is a witness.

Knowledge is power, so it is good to know these things and not always rely on what you are told.

Take note of this, especially for people in Lagos, Nigeria, do not buy land from the self-acclaimed indigenous owners (*omo onile*) because they will not give you any of the essential titles, they will only give you a receipt, and this does not transfer title it's just evidence that payment was made. Buy from a credible real estate company

Approach credible real estate companies like Gtext Homes that have offices all over the world and have a reputation to protect. We have built multi-billion naira real estate assets in Nigeria with over 20 estates, and we're building the largest luxury estates in the world. We have several of our estates in Lagos, both on the mainland and Island, Abuja, Abeokuta, Ibadan, Asaba, Port Harcourt, Dubai, the U.K., and the U.S.

You are indeed in safe hands when you buy property from Gtext Homes. The company sends your documents to you anywhere worldwide immediately after payment is made. You can make payments through the company's mobile app using your card, even for those paying by instalments.

Note: You have to pay to process your Survey and Deed of Assignment. The standard price for a Lawyer to prepare a Deed of Assignment is ten percent of the price of the land while a Surveyor does the survey. Get your documents so you have full authority over your land.

Gtext Homes is into service plots. A serviced plot is one in which the developer will provide the road, fence, security, electricity, running water and every form of infrastructure. As a result, a serviced plot value always appreciates more than typical plots.

NOTABLE QUESTIONS

Is there any difference between an Agreement and a Deed of Assignment?

An Agreement is a document between you and the seller explaining the property, the terms of selling the property, and payment terms. It's an MOU (Memorandum Of Understanding), a mutually agreed document that states the details of a transaction; it does not transfer ownership. What, by law, transfers ownership is the Deed of Assignment.

Is there a difference between a Deed of Transfer and a Deed of Assignment?

We have the Deed of Conveyance, Deed of Transfer, and Deed of Assignment. There are different terms used in different situations, so it's just terminology based on the peculiarity of the property being purchased.

What is the difference between a Provisional Survey and a Registered Survey?

A Provisional Survey has not been registered with the Ministry of Lands, while a Registered Survey has been registered with the Ministry of Lands. It takes a registered surveyor to produce a Registered Survey, but the seller usually gives you a Provisional Survey.

To understand how real estate works, land with a plan or structure will always appreciate compared to one without.

Finally, there is power in owning property, but you cannot build wealth if you are not humble.

CHAPTER 5
How To Become A Land Banking Billionaire I

I'm not big on keeping money in the bank; instead, investing. So, as I make more money, I keep buying properties. Some of those secrets are what I'm sharing with you in this book. One of the things I keep educating people on is that it is never overnight. When we often mention the subject of billions, people are quick to ask how they can do it fast and quickly. Many people have reached out to me asking, "How do I make money quick and fast?" and the reply I give them is, "I don't know". And I mean it. I have never been lucky in my life; I don't know what luck is. I had to go through a process of building wealth in my life; it wasn't sudden. I am not one of the people who got it through quickly. I wish I had the opportunity to teach you quick ways to make wealth.

Land banking is one of the best ways to become wealthy legally. In Nigeria, there is no better way to build wealth without soiling your name or becoming corrupt. You don't need to become a crony of political parties or people in government. But, it's one of the ways you can build wealth and be proud of it, such that years later, you can look back and say, "I'm proud of what I've done; I don't have to collect government money or steal money meant for road construction and social amenities to build wealth."

"Land appreciates, even while you sleep."

The landlords make more money even when they are sleeping. If you buy land genuinely from the right source, you don't need to do something on it for the value to appreciate. If you choose to do something like I do, then the value of that property appreciates much faster, and you'll have much to benefit from. But you do not need to do that. Even if you buy the land and you're able to have partners who ensure that your land is secure, you are guaranteed to be wealthy just by having land. So, this is a powerful way many people can come out of poverty using, and it works. It can also work for you if you want to do something.

Let me give you the story of a man called Pastor Paul Adefarasin. If you don't know him, Google his name and check. I have shared this story multiple times. His father was a Civil Servant in Lagos State. He retired, and they gave him 2000 pounds as gratuity. In those days, Nigeria spent Pounds. He used the £2000 to buy land at Victoria Island, precisely, Akin Adesola. Before you say that Victoria Island is a good place, I want you to know that, in those days, Victoria Island was extremely marshy, and people were unwilling to buy it. The highlight cities in Lagos State (as of then) were Yaba, Mushin, Berger, Ojuelegba, and Isale Eko. Research revealed that.

Victoria Island was being avoided because it was marshy, there was water around it, and nobody wanted to stay there. These are the things people don't know. I've seen people saying that they would have done what others did if they were in their shoes, not realising that opportunity always comes like a lousy market, and the reason why you are not taking advantage of the opportunity coming your way now is that they don't look like they are opportunities. They are looking like wrong moves; you're unsure. "What's the guarantee it would work?" So, you're not making the right move because you're not sure it's the right move.

Years later, many people started moving to Victoria Island when it became a land bubble. There is something called a land bubble in land banking. Right now, the place where there is a land bubble in Lagos State is called Ibeju-Lekki. Every season, there's always a place where there is a land bubble, where everyone wants to get something. In those days, Victoria Island was the land bubble, but his father had bought that land before Victoria Island became a land bubble. So, a company came to his father requesting to build on his land. They said they would take the rent of the house they built on the land for ten years, make back their money, get the money, and return the ownership to him. The man agreed. Some of you would not have agreed if you were in his shoes. You would be afraid, unsure if they would cheat you. Many people are always afraid and not wanting to take risks.

"Investment is about risk, but it is risky not to take risks."

He agreed, and they built on it. True to their words, they returned the land as agreed. The profit from that land banking was used to send all of his children to one of the finest institutions in the world. Aside from that, after his father died 50 years later, the land bought for 2,000 pounds was sold for about five million dollars. That is what we are talking about when we say there's money in this business model. So, it would be best if you took seriously what I'm teaching you in this book. You can build wealth in this industry. It is a whole lot!

How Do You Become A Land Banking Billionaire?

I'll take it one step after the other such that you'll still understand even if you're not an expert. The model I'm teaching you is so detailed that you will be able to do it brilliantly. These steps are the steps I took, and the first is very critical. I implore you to take it seriously because you'll be glad you did it years later.

Step 1: Don't Buy One Plot! Just Don't!

I think this is one of the biggest mistakes people make. When starting your land banking journey, one of the biggest challenges you might likely face is the availability of adequate funding. Because of this, many do it almost reluctantly, more like a game of chance–let's see what happens. And so many people do not buy more than one plot. I'll tell you the danger of that. It puts you in a position where you look back and begin to regret your decision because if you had bought more than one plot, you would have achieved much more. I'm going to tell you a short story about a student who came for one of my real estate classes. His story is efficient and would help buttress my point.

He bought land in a very marshy place for twelve million naira. They used a canoe to take him to the land. That was 15 years ago. It was owned by Chevron cooperative, but the place is now known as NICON Estate. When he bought the land, he bought only one unit. He didn't know the land would appreciate so much, and fifteen years later; I was one of those who started marketing that land for him for 220 million naira; from 12 million to 220 million naira. That's the reality of this.

The day we went to the land, he said, "I regret not buying two plots." He said that was his biggest regret. He said the money he needed was barely 100 million. If he had bought two, he would have sold just one, take the N100 million, used the remaining N120 million to develop the second land, and probably started selling houses or renting them out. He said, "I regret not buying more. But you can't blame me; I didn't believe this place would appreciate this much; we used a canoe to come here. I couldn't step on the land because it was all water. It was because I had enough money with me then that I decided to get it, whether it worked. That was why I got the property. I never believed it could become this big."

That is always the mistake many of us make when we stumble into land banking. We didn't do it intentionally; it was just because we had some cash. And then, you see people buying an excellent location that years later, they regret they didn't buy more.

So the first rule is, if you're buying land for land banking, do not buy one; at least buy two plots, one acre or more. When the property eventually appreciates, it becomes so good that you may end up living there. Then, you can sell one and use the money to develop the other one.

Who knows tomorrow? The place you're buying now is bushy and marshy, there's water everywhere, and people are wondering if your head is correct. Don't mind them, buy two. If you're serious about building genuine wealth through land banking, it is wise to say to yourself, "I will buy at least two plots." Are you getting value? Are you learning?

Step Two: Keep The Land For At Least Five Years.

Another mistake I've seen people make is not keeping the land long enough for it to appreciate significantly. They're quick to sell it. Candidly, at least, could you keep it for 5 years? In buying properties, hunger would come, desperation would set in at some point, you'd need money for your family, and things would happen that you didn't plan for. I understand that we all pay bills. But do your best to close your eyes for at least 5 years without touching the land(s) you purchased.

For the man who bought land for 12 million naira and sold it for 220 million naira, if he sold that land 5 years after he bought it, he couldn't have sold it for more than 20 or 25 million naira. Do you agree? Perhaps, he would have sold it for approximately N40 million. But can N40 million naira be compared with 220 million naira? Would he have forgiven himself if he had hastily sold it for N40 million and later heard that land in that area was going for N220 million? I don't think so. He would have been full of regrets. These are the reasons you don't rush to make certain decisions. Because of temporary financial constraints, you rush and sell your parcel of land for a bowl of pottage. You've heard that story between Jacob and Esau where he sold his birthright for a morsel of bread. You don't want to be one of those sets of people.

Calm down; give it at least 5 years. You can decide not to wait for 5 years if you've improved on the land. For example, you bought land and decided to fence it throughout. As a result, you added some value to it immediately. At that point, you'll still be able to sell it for something because you've also added value to that property.

But in many cases of land banking, you only buy it from an open source and leave it for a while. Because if you immediately start selling it, you will lose. I assure you that you'd look back years later and start regretting why you sold it all.

You don't want to put yourself in a situation where you bought a suitable property and regret later that you were not patient. I've heard several people have this regret about their land banking investments because the property they sold for peanuts eventually became very big. I'm sure some of you have met people like that who sold their property too early. Of course, you don't want to sell too early, except you bought so much that you can sell part. But, keep it, for at least five years. Don't rush. Don't be one of those people who sell their fortune because they 'urgently need money.'

"Land banking is a long-term game, not a short time game." Every land banking professional knows that.

Step 3: Sell Half Of The Land After Five Years And Use The Money To Buy A New Plot.

You can sell half of the land after five years and look for a new location that is developing and suitable for land banking. In 5 years, the location you bought would have started taking shape, and new locations would have emerged that also have the potential for appreciation. So rather than wait, sell half of the one you bought and look for a new location that appreciates and ties something down there. Does this make sense to you?

That is how wealthy people create wealth. They are always ahead of time. *They continuously invest in properties, are conscious of locations, and always move fast.* The owner of Eleganza, Chief

Razaq Okoya, did this very well. I must commend him. He used to have his industrial estate at Lagos Tollgate. After a while, he moved to another location, Okota, and started buying more of Okota. In another season, he moved to Lekki, but he used the Lekki investment to build more residential estates. Now, he has moved to Epe (with his industrial estate in Epe). This is how intelligent people always go ahead of time. They see into the future and peg the opportunities in it. They don't wait till it happens.

The third move is to sell half of the land and look for another promising location to purchase. At that point, you can as well use some money to start building residential accommodation in that location.

These are powerful ways to build wealth and become a land banking billionaire. You want to act fast! You want to take them quickly, and be very proactive in your moves.

Step 4: Use Evidence Of Your Property Purchase To Attract OPM

OPM means 'Other People's Money'. So you have to use other people's money. And the way you can use other people's money in a land investment is to prove to them that you also bought yourself.

Many people find it difficult to use OPM when it comes to landed properties because they are trying to sell the land they have not used their money to buy. Imagine you're trying to convince your friends to buy a particular land in Ibeju-Lekki, and they ask you if you've bought it yourself, and all you can say is, "Don't bother about that; the place is good." At that point, you lack what we call 'Credibility'.

How can you tell me, your friend, to do something you've not done before? For you to have not found the money to have invested in the land, why are you then telling me to invest in it? That is one of the biggest mistakes many property brokers make. So, after you have bought, one of the most significant ways to raise money to keep buying more land is to become a property broker. But always use the evidence of the one you bought to convince your friends and loved ones to buy. If I'm telling you to buy property in Ibeju-Lekki, know I own a property there.

People always ask me how I sell very well. Sometimes I sell up to 10, 20, or even 50 plots in one day. It is because people trust me. Why do they trust me? They know I've used my money to buy the land. If you're buying one plot, one acre, etc., I have used my money to buy 100 acres in that place. So, you're more comfortable trusting me because I was the first person who got there, and you know I wouldn't have put my money if I was not convinced there is potential in that location. Many of you do not know that once you have bought land, you have earned the credibility to sell to people, and an average company gives you a commission of 10%, 5%, 15% or 12% on every land bought through you.

Becoming wealthy is always a function of residual income. That extra token, 1% here, 2% there, or 5% there, is not a function of your active income. It is a mighty move when you get a percentage from another person's effort. That is how to make wealth. It's a powerful strategy that people have used repeatedly and has always worked–OPM. But it will be challenging to use other people's money by telling them to come and invest if you've not built credibility by proving you've bought the land with your own money.

So, when you convince your friends to buy land, you get a commission which you can use to purchase more land. If I buy one plot and convince 10 of my friends to buy, and I get a 10% commission on them, that gives me enough money to get one extra plot. Suppose I combine 50 people; that gives me enough money to get extra five plots.

"This is how you can acquire more land with other people's money instead of your money."

The mistake you make is that instead of buying the land first and convincing your family members and friends to buy through you, you first tell them about your intentions, and when they ask where and you reply that it's in Nigeria, they'd go, "Ah! Don't do it!" And they convince you against your intentions. No, it would help if you bought it first. That's what I did; all my family members are on my neck to buy properties from my company. If I had told them I wanted to go into land banking, even my dad wouldn't have agreed because his brother escaped an assassination attempt thrice because of land issues.

Meanwhile, he's still alive and over 85. The lesson is that I waited until I had the result before telling family members. Then, when they saw the result, they couldn't discourage me again.

Many of us want to do great things in business and investments, but we first tell people we want to make a move. They put fear in us, and we end up not doing it, and we blame them if we realise that we should have done it in the future. Meanwhile, it was our fault. You should first do it, take the risk, and afterwards, tell people you know and convince them you also did it. As they do it, you earn a 10% commission which you can use to keep buying properties.

Step 5: Get A Mentor.

That is the final point, and it is essential. It's always wise to get somebody who has results in a business to mentor you. I always tell people it's wisdom. Don't be greedy, don't think you're clever. I tell people, "Business people do not always look clever. Entrepreneurs do not always look like they know what they're doing." That is because most entrepreneurs always pay dues. They share whatever they're making. For example, 15% of every money that comes into my company goes to brokers. 15% of the entire income is distributed among those who bring companies to our company. If I had made 1 billion naira in a year, N150 million would have gone to brokers. And I'm not talking of contractors or vendors; I mean those who brought somebody.

That is how wealth is created. But when you meet an average poor man, he doesn't want to share his profits with anybody. He wants to eat it alone. So he's always like, "I can do it by myself; what's the big deal there?"

You need to get a mentor; if you don't have a mentor, how do you know the right place to buy one? How do you even secure the land? Because land banking is usually buying a piece of property with the potential to appreciate. You need a mentor to show you this. When you buy land, how do you make sure it doesn't get taken from you? You need a mentor to show you how. Mentors play a critical role in helping you to build massive wealth. That's how you get wealthy. Use a mentor's help.

I know of a friend of mine who started this business with just N350 million, he's now a big guy. He's based in the U.S. He got a partner in Nigeria; the partner doesn't have money, but he has connections. He knows how to buy suitable land; he knows how to secure the land. He knows how to get labourers to fence the land around and things like that. This partner helped him. That is a true story. In the last four years, he has converted 350 million naira into 20 billion naira in land banking and house flipping. They do business models, land banking and house flipping. They buy a house, remodel it and then sell it.

He has built assets to 20 billion naira in four years from 350 million naira. But if this guy didn't partner with someone in Nigeria, who didn't even have money but knew how to do the business, he would have lost all his money. And this is where people get greedy. I was teaching in Baltimore three years ago. A woman said, "Dr Stephen, it's difficult for those of us in the diaspora to build wealth in Nigeria. I had a business in Nigeria before I relocated to the U.S. I left it in the hands of someone I trusted, and they've ruined that business today."

I smiled and replied, "With all due respect, ma, when you were leaving Nigeria, did you tell your partner? There's nothing wrong in calling the person you wanted to hand over to and asking him to purchase 15% equity in the business. Bring in an independent evaluator to evaluate the entire business and tell the person you want to hand over the value of the business, let's say 100 million naira. Tell him you're willing to sell him 15% equity of the business for 15 million naira. Tell him to raise the money from family and friends. Tell him that when you share the profit, he will keep 15% and that he's free to buy more than 15% if he wants. Ma, what's wrong with doing that?"

She replied, "That's true; it never occurred to me." So I told her that if she had done that, most likely, she would not have had that issue, and she agreed.

Many times if you get a mentor (a neutral person) to help you review the decisions you made, your steps and actions that made you lose money, you would realise that you also made some mistakes. But we often go into business with emotions and sentiments and without mentors. Even if a mentor advised you, you would tell him he's not related to you, so he should keep quiet. Many time, people play the victim; the reality is that they played sentiments years ago. "He is my cousin, nephew, and in-law." they had the opportunity to have gotten a neutral person. Even the partner of the guy I was telling you about is not in any way related to him. So, he did it purely based on knowing the guy had a track record and integrity, and it was based on the guy's merit.

Our company is doing so well because everything is based on merit, equity and justice. You can rise from nobody in Gtext Holdings and become the number one person, no matter who you are and where you are from, as long as you have the result to show. That's how companies and businesses grow. You cannot become nepotic. There are no family members in my business, and nothing is wrong. If I find a family member qualified to work in my company today, I will hire them, but I've not found one.

So, building a system based on results, track record and what people can bring to the table is how you build a great empire for yourself.

FREQUENTLY ASKED QUESTIONS

a. Can I Partner With Someone To Acquire Land?

Answer: There is a tie response to that question. Before people become your partner, you need to make sure you share the same values and build mutual trust. So, you can partner, especially if it's divisible, perhaps 50:50. Even if we fight, I can write to the company that sold it for us to separate the land or give us a separate document. Always go to relationships that are easy to settle disputes if they arise. There's a land case that happened with a Pastor.

I didn't get to hear his part of the story, but the little I heard has it that there was a love affair mixed with buying of land. And what I tell people is to separate their love life from business. Let them be purely separate. I have fired my wife from my company before. Yes, I fired her and established her in another company. My family members know that I don't play with business. My younger brother, our last born, spent just 24 hours in my company. He sought a job, got the job and started stories that don't make sense to me, such as "Big brother, allow me to be closing early." It doesn't make sense to me; it's a company, not a family business, not Akintayo and Sons. So, separate love and family life from business. And, I only hire people I can fire. I will never give you a job if I can't sack you. I will never employ you if I know that I can't fire you for any reason. So, from the day I employ you, I already know that you are sackable; I can fire you clear-cut without issues.

Secondly, if you're receiving money from people, open a Limited Liability Company separate from your person. For example, if you buy land from me as the Managing Director of Gtext Homes, if there are issues, it is Gtext Homes you had business with, and you have all right to seek all entitlement from Gtext Homes. It cannot even affect me. That's why you'll see two people in a court sitting and talking in America. Their lawyers will come and still, find a way to resolve issues. In developed countries, they have learnt to separate personal issues from business. But when we mix these things, we create a mess of bitterness, envy and jealousy. I always separate my relationship with people from Gtext Homes. Some of my friends get contracts from Gtext Homes, but I ensure I am not the one on the board who approves their contracts. So, they come to me and say, "Dr Stephen, I'm a building contractor; I can help you build this and that." I direct them to the company's email address info@gtexthomes.com for application. I will tell them I don't have a say, and actually, I don't have a say. I don't choose contractors for Gtext Homes. So, you'll face the board and prove that you can do the job, not that you'll come to show them you're the friend of the boss. These are powerful principles that help guide business relationships. Let your friends know that you don't mix business with sentiments.

b. Do You Think There Could Be Bubble Land On The Mainland?

Answer: Yes. Ikorodu is a bubble land. During EndSars, some people who were very good at swimming said they just jumped into the lagoon close to Oriental Hotel, and landed in Ikorodu. In fifteen minutes from Ikorodu, you're on Victoria Island. As soon as a road and bridge connects that Lagoon straight to Ikorodu, I promise you, the most giant bubble in Lagos will be in Ikorodu.

The land bubble started in the mainland in Ikeja when Jakande started housing estates. So, there had been a landing bubble in the mainland, and there is still a land bubble in the mainland; it's just where you look. Abule Egba was also a big land bubble. There are always land bubbles from time to time, and Ikorodu is the next; that's why I invested a lot in Ikorodu. Soon, you'll know how much I've done in Ikorodu.

c. Do You Think There Can Be A Strict Standard Structure Area For Country Homes And Plans In Lagos?

Answer: The country home is usually about having mass land, and if you have the money, there is nothing you can't do in Lagos. Some people have country homes in Ikoyi.

d. Do You Involve A Lawyer When Buying Land With A Partner?

Answer: This 'involving lawyer' thing is neither here nor there. As I said, I have friends who come to bid for jobs in our company. The people they talk to are not lawyers; it's just about putting standards that spell out what we're doing. So, whether lawyers are involved, things have to be done correctly. For example, if you're buying properties from our company, no matter who you are (even a family member), there is a form you'll fill out, and you'll have your receipt. A contact is prepared. That one takes three to six months, but they prepare your Deed of Assignment, and a Survey is done for you. There is a structure; you can't come back later and start giving stories. There are records to show if you're buying the land in instalments. Every client has a file. So, if you're not done paying your money, and you're lying that they didn't give you land, there are records to show. Just putting proper process is what is essential.

It's not bad if you involve a lawyer, but you need to know what you're buying yourself rather than relying too much on lawyers. There was a property I wanted to buy. Thank God I was involved in the whole negotiation and did my independent research before I told my lawyer to prepare the documents. At the point of him preparing the documents and taking the cheque to the person I was buying from, my lawyer told them that unless the family gave him something, he would frustrate the deal. Thank God those people had direct access to me and had to say it to me. That is why I tell people you can involve lawyers, but know what you're trying to do instead of putting the whole thing on lawyers. The trust people had for families, they've pushed it on lawyers now. And we fail to realise that humans will always be humans, whether they are lawyers or not. Absolute power corrupts. So, when you put all the power on a lawyer, you have made the wrong move. I had to remove the lawyer from the deal for us to complete the deal.

Some people buy properties from Gtext Homes and ask to involve their lawyers. We've had a scenario where the lawyer insisted that 10% of his charge must be paid to him; else, he would tell the client not to go ahead and transact with Gtext Homes. We have seen a lot. Just know what you're doing very well and try to recognize the companies that uphold integrity. I would rather do business with a man with integrity without any lawyer present than with a man who does not have integrity with the best lawyer present. If the person doesn't have integrity, even if I bring all the lawyers in the world together, if he's going to be dishonest, he would still be dishonest. My lawyers would say they would fight him, but don't forget that lawyers only want to get their fees. The best and most intelligent people do not have issues that degenerate and lead to quarrels.

Remember the story of the wisest King Solomon. The Bible says he had many armies and kept building houses for his army but never went to a single war. That's wisdom. It's better to have lawyers and not use them than to keep going to court every day. It never helps anybody to settle.

Now, how do you know people are credible? Check their track records. How long have they been in the business? Have they been consistent? It's easy to know these things, but unfortunately, many of us prefer to buy something cheap rather than expensive and expensive. People lament that my properties are expensive; they go elsewhere and return crying that they were jilted. Isn't it better to buy something expensive and worth it than be cheated? If I know I'm giving something valuable, I charge you decently for my services. People who always sell to you at a low price do that because they know they will not sell to you simultaneously. Someone asks how he's going to know a credible mentor. It's the same thing. Does he have results? He is teaching real estate; how many estates does he have? I'm qualified to teach you today. I have over 15 estates in Lagos, Abuja, and Ogun State, and I'm expanding to 200. It's not a theory. Many of us pick mentors who do not have results. Again, you need to know someone like me would not be cheap. You can't meet me and say, "Dr Stephen, mentor me for free." How? Where? Did I learn what I learnt for free?

I have made hundreds of millions of losses in real estate before I can now teach you so that you won't make those losses. Don't you think I deserve to charge you a token to teach you how to not lose the kind of money I have lost and how to do things safely? Don't you think it is wise that you can even come under my wings and do business directly with my company? These are things that are important that we understand.

e. Dr Stephen, When Are You Going To Invest In Ijebu Land?

Answer: Property in Ijebu does not appreciate like that of Lagos, so I've not invested. The only place where the property is exciting in Ijebu is Sagamu. Sagamu is becoming better. When it comes to investment, stop being sentimental. It would be best if you did not necessarily buy land from Ijebu because you are from Ijebu. I'm from Egba in Abeokuta, but I don't have a plot there. Do you know why? The land does not appreciate yet. If I see signs that properties have started appreciating there, I can use nativity privileges.

I'm considering investing in Ogun State just because of the World Bank report that Ogun State is doing well and investors are gradually moving there. I'm gradually considering investing in some parts of Ogun State. A savvy businessman does not do business based on sentiments like 'my town, my village, where I hail from...' The question should be, "Where do I put my money, and will I get good returns?"

So, you look at the reports, ease of doing business and areas where there will be returns on investment, etc.

CHAPTER 6
HOW TO BECOME A LAND BANKING BILLIONAIRE II

How to make, manage, multiply money, and transfer the funds to the next generation.

In this chapter, we will continue discussing how to become a land banking billionaire. I hope you are ready to learn.

I have always said that I dislike relationships with people who are not hungry for success. Success is possible for all who desire it, but you must be hungry and thirst for it! Those who are not hungry for success cannot make it. Anything you tolerate has the right to remain. You should not be comfortable with your current level; you should be hungry for more.

Some people say poverty is no big deal. They must be kidding. Who sold that lie to you? May you never have a cause to lose your mother to ovarian cancer because you could not take her to a good hospital that would adequately take care of her before you realise there is nothing to be proud of about poverty. Hate it! Fight it! And do everything it will take you to come out of it! That's how to get wealthy. But if you think there's no big deal about poverty and only God knows who will be rich, that reveals that you are nonchalant about wealth creation.

Can I tell you, it's a big deal being poor? So many of us are poor because we are not hungry for wealth; we are not hungry for success; we're just comfortable.

My kids have the kind of life I never had; they have the best kind of life because their father worked hard to escape poverty. You have to do the same. My kids will not just love me today; they will love me in years to come; they will remember what I have done and look back at my real estate investments. They will kiss my picture and tell their children to thank God for grandpa.

Not only will you make money legitimately, but people will also talk about the good things you have done, the value you have added, and how you made a change because you decided to be responsible.

When we talk about wealth and entrepreneurship, people think it's just all about money, but a significant part of it is also about the impact you have made so that the world can remember you as one of those who change their world for the better.

This book is not a get-rich-quick medicine because I didn't get rich quickly either. This is my fifteenth-plus year owning my business. It has been fifteen years of not giving up. It is about knowing the principles and following them consistently.

It takes time to grow wealth, there were lands I bought seven years ago for 750,000 naira, and today it is worth 10 million naira. So you see that it takes time, but it is accurate and works. I could have bought crypto, and it crashed at some points, and I could have traded forex and lost everything too. However, I ascertain that it stays consistent for real estate if you buy it from an authentic source and genuine people.

So, you already know what land banking is from the previous chapters. Still, to recap the definition of land banking, it is the practice of buying land as an investment, holding it for specific future use, such as for reselling or developing it - I did both for some of the lands I bought. For example, I bought 50 acres of land some years back and decided to sell 20 acres from it and build on the rest. The money I made from my sales is what I am using to build on the ones I decided to develop. So I made money from selling and will still make money from building. That is how it operates. Land banking is about buying at least 3 plots for a start. You can buy as much as you can, depending on your financial capacity.

I sold one of our properties here in Dubai recently. This land was bought at a minimum cost in the 90s by an Indian man. The land was so cheap when he got it; today, as I speak, my team sold just two units of 75 hectares from the land for 20 million dollars. That is what happens in land banking.

Do you know that all the wealthiest people today are into land banking? Land banking is one of the surest ways of building and transferring wealth to the next generation.

Today, Shanghai–China, sells air rights. For example, a man owns a 50-floor building, so, as a developer, you will go to the man and tell him you want to buy from the 50th floor to the 80th floor. That is how lands are sold in China. They do not sell ground anymore. This is the beauty of land banking, such that in the nearest future when lands are no longer there to sell, you will begin to sell air space. This is the power of real estate.

Do you know that just two categories of people are called lords in the world–the Landlords and the Judges? The landlord is the land owner, and the other is the judge of the land. So, you are influential on your land. That's why when God wants to bless people with prosperity in Christianity, he gives them lands as possessions. So, you are not yet rich until you own your property.

You are taking Dubai as another case study. In 1991, Dubai was purely a desert, but today, it's another story entirely. All the empty spaces we advertise today as our estate, watch out for the space; in 30–40 years to come, you will be shocked at what they will have become. I had to study land banking at Harvard University to understand the nooks and crannies of real estate. If you want to be very rich, you should consider real estate.

"Do the impossible with the available."

Starting a real estate business costs a lot, and sometimes you will wonder if you have made the right decision; it would look like you are struggling, but you must not give up because you know where you are going. That's how we started too.

One of my students shared how he had acquired 500 plots of land within one year; such a person has created wealth for his coming generation. One of the richest men in the world, McDonald, owns a burger company, but he makes more money from land banking than his burger business. For every McDonald's shop you see, they own the land. He gets the land and leases it out to their franchises, making money from there. I hope you are getting value.

McDonald is a real estate company, and the only reason they sell hamburgers is that it is the most significant producer of revenue from which their tenants can pay them their rent.

I have a strong passion for helping people and have been criticised repeatedly, including on social media, but I have made up my mind never to give up. So, you will be talked down and criticised, but never allow that to stop you from your goals. They are just distractions you mustn't pay attention to if you want to impact your world. When I see the testimonies of people whose lives have changed through us, it encourages me to keep going.

Some people have vowed that they are not going to be somebody important in life, and those are people who pull down others who are on their way to rising, so we will not allow those who are determined to make it to be affected by others who do not want to make it.

What Are The Benefits Of Land Banking?

The first is **Long-Term Appreciation**. That means the land property continues to appreciate for as long as you leave it. Another benefit is that of **a Low Entry Point**. That means it's a lot cheaper to start land banking compared to buying a house property. Your buying or building a house property for profit-making needs constant maintenance. But for land property, you do not need any maintenance; after buying, you can leave it for as long as you wish if you purchase it from a credible real estate company. The third benefit discussed here is **Maximum Flexibility**. It is one of the major benefits of land banking.

There are significant characteristics that distinguish Real estate from other economic resources.

1. Fixed location
2. Uniqueness
3. Interdependence of land uses
4. Long life
5. Long-term commitment
6. Large transaction
7. Long gestation period.

Real estate is long-term, so all this short-term thinking and short-term money are not the way to land banking.

What unique characteristics give local comparative advantage for certain uses – what are the key things to look at, and where are the good places to do land banking? Also, how do you identify the right land banking opportunities?

1. Nearness to good transportation facilities: Buying land close to major transportation facilities is a good place.

2. Educational facilities: By investing in lands close to a major university or certain secondary schools, you are making the right decision.

3. Created environment: This is what Gtext Homes is doing today. In all our estates, we have unique facilities such as Golf courses and Polo clubs.

4. Natural Resources: For example, one of our estates is close to the sea. Because of its proximity to the sea, Dangote decided to bring a refinery company there. Now, because of these unique resources, there needs to be more housing, particularly quality

housing for the expatriates. Also, a seaport is situated close to the refinery, and some people like to live closer to the beach, so we currently have three estates that are close to the beach.

5. Labour force: This is still part of the Dangote refinery. Because of all this amazing infrastructure coming to Ibeju-Lekki, the labour force has increased. Dangote alone has employed over 57,000 people, of which 15,000 are expatriates. That has created a situation where people need houses and land. Property prices are on the high side, more companies are moving in, and property value is also increasing. The land we sold for N1.5 million in 2019 at the Ibeju-Lekki axis is currently going for N15 million because of the labour force and climate.

6. Leadership: Check out for things like the developers of that place. Before investing in them, you must vet the brand and ensure they are trustworthy and dependable. In Gtext Homes, apart from me as the MD, the then COO was a well-certified real estate developer. He has over 20 years of experience with many certifications, so he is an expert. The last project he handled before he joined us at Gtext Homes was a 102-story building project, so you should be sure he is very competent and reliable. You see me bold publicly because I am confident of our output.

7. Local Law and Regulations: In Nigeria, local laws may not necessarily support it, but there is a huge housing deficit in Nigeria–over 20 million. Lagos alone has almost 20 million occupants, and according to the Washington Post, the population of Lagos state by 2100 will be around 80 to 100 million people. The land size wouldn't increase, so

where would people live? So, you are wealthy if you own land in Lagos. In addition, Lagos has the highest return on investment in Africa. These are the things you consider, not just buying any land.

How Do You Start Your Estate?

1. Determine what you want to be known for. Have a unique idea; you cannot be everything, define your audience, research the industry, ask for reviews and understand how the business works, prepare an elevator pitch, embrace networking, join a community, ask questions and ask for recommendations. Instead, grow your brand offline and online, and organise meetings where you meet people and get to know more about them.

I end with this; ***if your net worth is not changing, change your network.*** The people you make friends with should be people who are making progress intentionally.

Warren Buffett said the best investment you can make is an investment in yourself. The more you learn, the more you earn. If you don't invest in growth, you cannot become wealthy.

Also, to be richer financially is to have been richer mentally. In other words, the richer you become mentally, the richer you become physically, so your physical wealth is a function of your mental wealth. Rich people use debt to leverage investment and grow cash flow, and poor people use debt to buy things that make the rich richer. Also, poor people buy what they don't need to impress people who don't care.

Bill Gates said, "If you're born poor, it's not your fault; but if you die poor, it's your mistake". So now that you are born poor, you must come out of poverty. It's not easy; you have to take the risk, which is tough.

Do you know that poor people remain poor because they hate

to take risks? Nobody made it on the first attempt. When you fail at some point, you try again until it works. This is how wealth is built, and that's how we got here. It's unfair when you see rich people and think they are lucky. I am not too fond of when people tell me I'm lucky because I know I'm not. I failed in almost 20 businesses before I finally made it in Real Estate. Elon Musk failed at some points, and Donald Trump bailed him out. On a live global television platform, Alibaba was once called a scam, but today he owns one of the biggest E-commerce businesses in the world. They all took risks, and they failed but rose and continued.

It is risky not to take a risk. The biggest mistake you will make in life is not taking risks. If you fail, move on and do not bring around yourself pity party people. In this same real estate business, I have failed and lost money. But I didn't quit, I continued, and today, God has made me a billionaire from it. I pray that you will make it, so do not give up.

Finally, you are the prophet of your destiny, so start speaking about what you want to see in your life. No matter what you are seeing, start speaking positive things about yourself, your life, and your business. It's not always easy, but keep saying what you want to see. No matter how tough everything seems, keep saying positive things – I'm going places, doors are opening, things are working, we're moving mountains, and the business is changing. Just keep saying it. Never depend on a single source of income; make investments to create the alternative, and one of those investments is land banking.

Today is hard, tomorrow will be worse, but the day after will be sunshine. So as you start your land banking business, it may seem harsh at first, but the latter will be great.

Here are a few questions and answers you can learn from.

Question 1: I have a new startup idea to solve the housing deficit crises in Nigeria, but nowhere to pitch the idea and get funding; it will be best if I can pitch it to you.

Answer: I no longer hear people's ideas. The reason is that the idea you are talking about, I probably have it already, and it may be that I do not have the money to execute it yet. Many ideas people talk about are money related, and all of us are looking for money. My advice is this: find a starting phase for your idea; you do not need to pitch it to anyone. People no longer fund ideas; people fund what they have started. Start as a property broker, and as you make money, start small. As you grow the business, people like us will look for you and tell you, let's partner together. I have had situations where people share ideas with me, and I have the same idea. Then, they will say Dr. Stephen stole my idea when I start executing it.

Question 2: How do I manage land grabbers?

Answer: First, never purchase any property from land grabbers. Land grabbers always sell the same land to more than one person. Please buy it from the right people. It may be more expensive, but it will save you the stress of land grabbers.

PART TWO
THE WEALTH OF SUSTAINABLE MENTORSHIP

CHAPTER 7

The Basics for Realtors: 5 Land Banking Lessons from Chief Razaq Okoya

"Show me a successful individual, and I'll show you someone who had real positive influences in their life. I don't care what you do for a living—if you do it well, I'm sure someone is cheering you on or showing you the way. A mentor."

— Denzel Washington

Meet The Manufacturing Giant

Born on the 12th of January, 1940, to the family of Tiamiyu Ayinde and Alhaja Idiatu Okoya, Chief Razaq Okoya has grown to become a torch for many industrialists across the globe. For every parent, the fate of their child(ren) is always of paramount concern, and they seek to talk out their hearts to the Creator in their limitations. One could almost tell that such was the case with Chief Razaq's parents as they could never have imagined that a day would come in the life of their son–Razaq Akanni Okoya–when he would become the sole employer of more than 4,500 employees.

Growing up, his reason for not pursuing a formal education beyond primary school–Ansar Ud Deen Primary School–was not far-fetched. His teachers in school looked nothing like the fly and well-padded business people of Lagos at that time, who had their heads up while carrying their briefcases, which almost seemed to be loaded with their business acumen. This led him to take a giant step of loaning an amount of 50 pounds from his mother (with his father's consent) with the sole aim of summing it up with the 20 pounds he had saved while amending clothes for folks in his father's tailor shop. With this capital, his journey into entrepreneurship began at age 17 as an importer of goods from Japan into his country–Nigeria. Due to his ability to explore beyond his borders, the manufacturer in him arose and saw the need to become more of a problem solver for his fellow citizens than an importer.

Furthermore, he was able to dive deeper into discovering the core problems that needed to be solved. The answer to this started Chief Razaq Akanni Okoya's journey into the world of renowned industrialists. It is 60 years after, and his locally manufactured goods have brought his presence into the homes of, if not all, almost all Nigerians. However, the epileptic power supply and government regulations have not always been favourable for Nigerian industrialists, who, in their resilience, keep finding means to gain and retain stability. For Chief Razaq Okoya, real estate was his go-to.

In my journey to becoming a successful land banker, time would fail me to explain to you the amount of time I have invested in studying the likes of this prestigious man. During my adventure in bringing wisdom from this manufacturing giant, I observed and discovered 5 land banking lessons that work for everybody and anybody. Out of sheer generosity, I decided to share them with you in this book. If you want to know, keep reading on. If you already have an idea, you can tell there's always more than you know. Are you not interested? Dear reader, neglected knowledge is a grand opportunity missed. Folly is such an act. This book is just for YOU!

Lesson 1: Buy That "Rejected" Property

Perhaps, you wonder, "What is land banking?" Land banking means purchasing undeveloped lands for the significant purposes of appreciation, investment, and sales once that land has been appreciated. That is the concept of land banking.

Do you know that many industrial plants or companies in

Oregun, Ikeja, and Lagos states, are owned by Chief Razaq Okoya? In those days, there were many manufacturing companies in the country, contrary to the good number of them we have today. However, the number one lesson I have learned while observing the highly industrial man from afar (specifically in land banking) is that he always goes against the crowd, trusting in turning the bush into a city. Thus, Chief Razaq started purchasing lands in places like the Oregun-Ikeja axis, Isolo, Alaba, Iganmu, etc. That was when Jakande was the governor of Lagos state. He tried to convince the civil servants to move and live in places like Abiola MKO Gardens and other estates. Chief Razaq bought those lands and built lots of estates. Unfortunately, many civil servants expressed disinterest due to a lack of insights. I could remember an eighty-four old retiree who was a civil servant who told me about how they condemned the idea with the "God forbid" vibe when persuaded to move to the then underdeveloped Ikeja. They would prefer the then governor, Jakande, and his family to move to such places.

However, rather than seeing this as a disadvantage or limitation, Chief Razaq Akanni Okoya saw opportunities to create transgenerational wealth and attain financial stability beyond manufacturing. Thus, his first strategy was to go against the popular opinion and trust in the concept of turning the bush into a city, such that when folks were avoiding Ikeja and its fellow underdeveloped neighbouring areas due to the thickness of the bush–more or less a forest, he kept investing and purchasing more lands. Initially, he intended to expand his industrial empire, manufacturing plants, etc. However, one of the unique things Chief Razaq did was acquire more lands than only he could use. As such, he could also sell vast expanses of land to his friends, who were equally industrialists and were also into manufacturing. He would have them approach him, request manufacturing plants, and have prepared for the future; he would sell to them. With this, his journey into the real estate world began.

Unfortunately, an incident took place in the 90s and early 2000 that had many manufacturing industries in Nigeria shut down on production, and Eleganza Group of Companies was at the centre of that intense heat. However, his company could transit and survive that massive blow because of the decisions he made many years ahead. He kept becoming richer. Many began to wonder how his financial tides were swimming against the manufacturing plants that kept shutting down almost daily. And for those that were still in operation, their production became minimal. That caused many to wonder and ask questions as he was no longer producing on the scale he used to. The answers to their questions weren't far-fetched. It was real estate! The lands he bought years ahead were greatly appreciated, and the location was well-developed. Folks started purchasing lands and warehouses from him, including the Daystar Church. People started buying warehouses, turning them into churches, and the Chief made huge sales. Development took over that entire area. As manufacturing companies were dying, including his own, baba could diversify heavily into real estate. Gradually, he sold most of these properties and kept making more money. Now, guess what his next move was? He moved to Lekki Epe and had The Eleganza Estate! The estate is located towards Ajah in Lagos State.

Thus, despite the challenges faced by manufacturing companies in the nineties and early twenties, Chief Razaq leveraged real estate. To become an excellent land banker, one must learn these powerful principles. One of the significant challenges Africans have faced viewing every wealthy individual as devilish or dubious instead of learning the core principles and strategies that worked for that individual. Regardless of the circumstance, I want you to know that a level will come when governments start transacting business and closing deals with people like Dr Stephen Akintayo. There is nothing I can do about that! When you grow to a level, it becomes purely government. It becomes

B2G. It's called Business to Government. So, while anybody can say what they want to me, reality still made the core of how I started my business. It was from grass to grace. Therefore, the fact that I'm now probably dealing with the government doesn't change the core basis of how I started humbly. Right? And in the long run, if any government decides to start partnering with Stephen Akintayo, does it delegitimize the fact that I worked my way extremely hard from the ground to the apex? Absolutely no! My story is a zero to hero one.

So, back to my conversation, baba went beyond the prevalent norms. He bought lands and built manufacturing complexes and warehouses in places people were not willing to go in those days. He built massive warehouses that could sell the warehouses even when manufacturing was an issue and moved to another location. This buttressed the points made by one of the founders of McDonald's when asked a very important question.

Now, let me say this, it is essential. One of the founders of McDonald's was once asked, 'You guys are in the business of selling burgers.' And he said, 'No, we're in the real estate business.' He further said, 'The reason is that in every location that we open McDonald's, even when we are no longer able to sell McDonald's when we sell those locations, we end up quadrupling. Sometimes, we have a 1000% return on investment. So, most of our big money comes from being able to sell most of our shops, should anything go wrong.'

Sadly, this is one of the strategies people sometimes fail to add to the business. However, I hope this book is delivering value to you already. So, the McDonald's co-founder said every location owned by McDonald's is a real estate focused. That explains the reasons for their moves, and it's even one of the crux of the success of McDonald's. Every McDonald's location is focused on real estate; if they cannot go ahead in the core business of selling burgers, that location is sold, thereby increasing their value and figures. In turn, they keep making more money. I have studied this principle in the life of Chief Razaq Okoya of Eleganza Group of companies and how he's been able to do that.

Lesson 2: Strategic Locations and Relocation

I must say that this generation needs to begin to learn from older people. Not all their acts were wrong. Everything is not bad about them. I was speaking with my female Executive Assistant on a particular day, asking her about her parents and all of that; she gave some reservations that made me laugh and comment on how the children of nowadays forget that the fact that you have certain reservations about your parents doesn't change them from being your parents. Period! It doesn't change the fact that they are good, and neither does it change the fact that they have good intentions. So while you may disagree now that you are old, don't forget that these people raised you when you didn't know your left from right. And I believe there are many lessons we need to learn from older business owners that can help us and put us in a better perspective moving forward.

My second takeaway lesson on land banking from Chief Razaq Okoya is location. Baba kept moving to new locations that had potential once the current locations were saturated. Do you know that Chief Razaq Okoya's central industrial hub has moved to Lekki-Epe? Are you aware of the Eleganza industrial estate in Lekki Epe? So, the same man who dominated the entire Oregun, with massive warehouses and manufacturing plants in Isolo and Alaba and Iganmu, suddenly relocated to another bush as soon as all these places became more saturated with people living in those areas. The bush was in Epe.

There was no point in keeping industry in Isolo or Oregun. They will constitute more pollution. That is because more development has already surrounded those locations, and these are intelligent concepts for wealth. Smart ideas! Land banking entails buying land in the bush, and then over time, you keep evolving and moving to where the future is. I studied how savvy baba did those things. I have estates along Lekki-Epe and Ibeju-Lekki. I am in awe of how bright and intelligent these people are each time! They saw the future, and they invested ahead. I mean, mediocre mindset individuals can sit somewhere and begin to debate and analyse these people and how it was because they have connections. Each time, I smile because if you understand how success works, there is no way you become successful to a level, and everyone won't want to associate with you, from the politicians to the government to the people in power. That's just how it works, and it has nothing to do with whether they are the ones supporting you or not.

In many cases, you give them money for their elections to support all of them, no matter what party they belong to. So, understand the powerful concept. I was in a virtual meeting where someone testified that he rented one of Chief Razaq's warehouses at Alaba 2 years ago. So, I hope you are flowing with me.

As such, Chief Razaq sold those properties and even moved his manufacturing plants from Oregun, Isola, Iganmu, and Alaba to another bushy location. Afterwards, what happened was that his presence in Epe turned the underdeveloped location into a developed one, and as those locations develop, he moves again. I must also inform you that I have over 1000 life-changing videos on YouTube with the channel name Stephen Akintayo. So you need to subscribe to my YouTube channel, as I have put a whole university for you.

Okay! Let's recap the number two lesson. Baba keeps moving when a location gets saturated; he moves to another location that is still bushy. He understands that with time, the bushy place will also develop. And once it has developed, baba would begin to sell gradually and make more money. He repeated the cycle of acquiring strategic locations and relocation again and again. That is one of the patterns some wealthy people use to reinvent themselves. And sometimes, it seems as though regardless of the happenings in the country's economy, these classes of people keep enjoying wealth. They keep looking big by the day. They keep making money and can sponsor a particular type of lifestyle. However, some who do not understand how these people have used strategies to build wealth can become jealous and pass disdainful comments at them. But then, this does not change the fact that these people used strategy and understood concepts. For Chief Razaq Of Eleganza Group of Companies, he kept moving and building other industrial complexes rather than getting all comfortable with a particular location.

The life of Chief Razaq Okoya buttresses the fact that everything big started on a small scale. His journey into the business world started humbly with just 70 pounds. Most of the wealthy people today were once poor. Perhaps, you might think that luck found them. That is outrightly incorrect. The story of your life that you so much despised is synonymous with how many of the great people you admire started, just like you. People do not become rich from heaven. They were poor before they made it. Whatever changed, their stories lie based on what they knew that got them to where they are today and knowing it lies in your ability to be hungry. To discover the secrets of rich people, admire them rather than despise them. You can never attract what you despise. If you hate rich people, you can't be rich. It's a simple, powerful law that works any day and anytime.

My first encounter with Chief Razaq Okoya was on the plane. We boarded the same plane from Germany to London. I could only greet him because we never really had time to converse. Although, over the years, I have observed and watched him do things from afar. More reason why I could package these 5 primary pieces of knowledge for your consumption in this book.

That will lead me to the third lesson.

Lesson 3: Engage your assets! They desire never to be idle.

Oh yes! Inland banking, it's best to find temporary residual income from your land banking, particularly when banking on a bulk scale. For example, if you buy either five or two acres of land, can you farm on it? Can you create an agricultural processing warehouse if you can't farm on it? Just find a way to start generating extra income from your land banking. Here's a typical example of what I noticed in Chief Razaq. Since Epe was quite a distance, like very far, I believe baba could have done another Eleganza estate as he did along Ajah, but he taught himself to meet the demands of too many people wanting warehouses from him in their previous locations and the demands are yet to be met. Besides, he had another consideration which was affordability. That resolved him to build another industrial estate in Epe, and some of them who didn't have much money rented warehouses or bought land and built their warehouses. He generated liquid from that place as development moved to the entire Lekki-Epe Expressway. Baba might use that estate again for commercial residents as things move down there.

Kindly note that this only works when you are doing bulk. If you buy one plot of land, there's no way you can probably monetize your 600 square metres. Well, there might be, but because it's land banking and the place is stiffer, you may not be able to do much there. But if it's larger, your two acres, five acres, and ten acres can build a warehouse upon which you can farm on the land, pending the time the whole place develops. You can as well build houses. For example, one of our estates in Ibeju-Lekki, Jasper estate, is very close to the Dangote refinery. Guess what? Because of that, we're already building houses. Our goal is that once we are done building the houses, we will write a letter to Dangote refinery, Power oil, Indomie, and all the companies that are in that axis, stating, "We have built readymade houses for your staff rather than have them live in temporary shelter or a far distance, as far as Ajah. As such, every morning down to Ibeju-Lekki, it will just be a 10 minutes drive from their abode to your refinery and plant. Can you start paying? This amazing concept will be fit for your staff".

Find some residual income, particularly when you do bulk land banking. The income might be little and not even make much sense. But, whether it is small money or not, let something be coming in. More reason why Chief Razaq Okoya is an outstanding industrialist; you can't take that from him. The man knows how to build manufacturing companies, warehouses, and real estate. He's just a giant, and there's a lot for young people like us to learn from people like that, okay?

I remember meeting a professor who is eighty five years old this year, and baba told me he almost cursed them when they gave him Surulere because, in those days, all those places were thick forests, and he was given five acres of land in Surulere. They were all bush; nobody lived there. Guess where people were living? Isale eko, Mushin, Ojuelegba, Ajegunle, etc. Those were the top core Lagos then. But look at how those places are called slums and suburbs now. You need to understand that turning a bush into a city is the entire concept around land banking, that is, being able to see into the future. If you're going to buy a bush now, buy it! Regardless of the location, Buy today! So stop planning or whining and buy! When you do, watch your children and great-grandchildren; thank you.

Listen, you can change the entire trajectory of your family and lineage with the land you buy today. You can change your life and destiny from a poor lineage to a rich one with just the property you buy. So let me share a real practical story with you guys.

Pastor Paul Adefarasin of House on the Rock Church replicated the same principle of his father as shared earlier in this book, and by the time the family decided, 50 years after, to sell the house after baba had died, the share of just one child was almost a million dollars.

Dear reader, do you now see how you can change your destiny and wipe away poverty from your lineage by buying one land? By just making that property investment decision? Like Pastor Paul Adefarasin's father, you can wipe away poverty from your lineage for life today! There is nobody from Pastor Paul Adefarasin's family that can be poor! How in the world? You can guarantee a roadmap or a strategy that nobody from your family will ever be poor again. With all sense of humility, with some of the investment decisions I'm making today, the following three generations of my family can't be poor, even if they waste money! Could you get it? Let's use Walt Disney as our subsequent case study.

Walt Disney built the wealth that once you are born into that family, you're a billionaire in dollars by just being born. You don't need to do anything! You're just a billionaire in dollars; no matter how wasteful you are, you cannot just finish billions of dollars like that. It doesn't just disappear.

Lesson 4: Diversify the purpose of your land banking investment. You must be flexible.

Diversify the purpose of your land banking investments. Some folks are too rigid and cannot maximise their land banking investment. You can sometimes buy land and use that land to build estates. In other words, you can build houses and rent them out. While in some cases, it can be that you bought the land only to resell the entire land after it has been appreciated. The point is, be flexible! You can buy land and convert it into a farm estate. Learn to be flexible as a land banker. That's what I noticed Baba did. Okay? For some locations, baba rented the warehouses out. He didn't sell it. For some locations, baba sold out the warehouses. While for some locations like the one close to Ajah, baba just built a residential estate. Even though that's not his core, he built a residential estate. For another location, baba decided to build an industrial estate. So, be flexible so that you can diversify your land banking investment. Do not be rigid, thinking that it must only be for farming or it must only be for building houses and renting them out alone. There are many things you can do with that house. It is either you build houses and sell them a house or rent it out. You can also do land banking and just farm on it or build a warehouse. Be flexible! Be willing to change! To adopt! When you have invested in land banking, be willing to adjust and adapt. Be flexible, my beloved reader!

Lesson 5: Make it a cycle. Consistently repeat the process.

Keep repeating the process. Do not ever give up on the concept of land banking. The moment you did it, and it worked, try it again. Secure another location to repeat the process. One of the biggest reasons people fail– and I've seen this across the globe– is that once they try something that works, they relax and stop repeating it. The hunger disappears. How sad can this be? So, I do something powerful, which is a decisive move, and I want to encourage you to do it intentionally. Okay, so I practise artificial brokenness. One of the most considerable harms you can ever do to yourself is to have too much money in the bank staring at you. Such that you become lazy. Money discourages effort. Let me repeat that powerful statement. MONEY DISCOURAGES EFFORT. I mean, there is a way you can have so much money in the bank that you become lazy. So, I practise artificial brokenness. Now, what do I do?

I have some money. Let's assume I have 500 Million Naira; I will embark on a project worth 1 Billion Naira. With that, I now need an additional 500 million naira urgently. What this does to you is that it gets you running. It gets you hungry and moving because you have to pay another 500 million naira, but some of you know what you do. With that, if you made 2 million, you're not leaving it in the account. You're not smiling. You want to be careful because you don't want to lose your money. Fear can sometimes cause you not to want to invest. The fear of losing your money. But then, how much of this money is in your account that you're afraid to lose? Instead of you saying money is a messenger. Money is supposed to be sent on an errand. You are not supposed to keep money in the bank. It is doing nothing. Inflation is eating the money up. The biggest enemy of investment is banks because the money you keep in the bank, the bank has used for business transactions.

Meanwhile, they will not give you a return on what they have used your money for. Do not allow the digits to deceive you into looking at paper money, thinking you have money. Inflation is hitting on that money, and that money is losing value.

What were you supposed to do? Invest it. Send it on an errand, such that you need more money. You've invested in something bigger than what you can afford. So you are hungry to keep generating income and expanding your investment empire; that is artificial brokenness. So, it's not like you don't have money; it's just that you send the money on errands. You sent the money to go and work for you and secure a better future for you and the next generation. As such, you're not discouraged from working harder.

At Gtext Homes, we have a slogan: *We do not just sell properties; we help you build your future.* And that's the truth! The guaranteed way to secure your future is to invest in property; it is to do land banking. If you do not go ahead and invest in land banking, property, investment, assets, etc., you will be poor. Not only will you be poor, but you have also transferred poverty to the next generation. Transferring wealth to the next generation is more honourable. I have vowed that I would transfer wealth to the next generation. I'm not going to transfer poverty to the next generation. I want to transfer wealth. I desire wealth to move from one generation to another. That is why it is called *transgenerational wealth.* If you are genuine about investing in real estate, be prompt about doing it. Invest in land banking. Here's one of the benefits of land banking that I want you to know; you can do it when you don't have much money. That's why we keep preaching land banking. You can start regardless of how little you have. It may just mean the land will not have documents yet, or it may still be in a thick forest. But by every means, invest in land banking! Do not forget to keep repeating the process that works. Keep repeating the process consistently.

One of the questions answered on my YouTube Channel–by the way, it is full of life-changing videos. Kindly advise them on whether you can invest in land banking with other people's money. I will never advise that you start land banking with other people's money because land banking is never short-term. Chief Razaq Okoya is 82 years old now. Imagine when he started buying all these lands, probably, 50 or 60 years ago or, let's say, 55 years ago. He started buying most of this land that had become gold in baba's hands because land banking is not a short-term project. Thus, please don't use other people's money until you have used your money to do it well. We've never even said anybody should come and invest in our company in terms of giving us their money so that we can use it to keep buying land and selling and give them profit. We never did it in three years because I needed to practise it repeatedly and be sure that I'd gotten a perfect model and that people would give me their money. I'll misuse it. I'll claim the victim. The owners of the money and I would have lost so much. Thus, I do not advise you to do that; instead, start small. All these people you see today started small.

You can copy that and start small, even with one plot. Start with 300 square metres. Start with Atan, Ibadan, Lagos-Ibadan express road, Mowe, Ofada, Arepo, Ibeju-Lekki, and Epe. Start somewhere! Start small! In some places, you buy land for 1 million naira with legitimate real estate companies. 1 million naira, 2 million naira, but make sure it is legit, right? But start small, and some of them will give you flexible payment. One of our estates in Atan is N1.2 million. You pay N500,000 and spread the rest. Start small!

Another way you can do this is to market for existing related companies that are credible. They give a 10 percent commission. You can then use that 10 percent commission to start buying your land. I know people who specifically told me to keep every money they make from selling our land to acquire their land. Since Baba was able to do something on the land rather than leave it as bare land, he either built a warehouse or residential accommodation or baba would do something. So, because he can do something on the land, there's just no way anybody can take it from him. He's already taken possession of his land, which is also why I advise that you buy from a real estate company. That is because real estate companies have security guards in all their estates. Real estate companies fence around their estates. Thus, you are sure your estate will be protected because of all these things. It's usually when you buy from *Omo onile* that you now have a real problem on your hands.

Avoid buying from *Omo onile.* So buy from a credible real estate company like Gtext Homes. That is the company I own. I'm the GMD of the company. Buy from us. We are not cheap, but we can assure you of our value. It is true that land banking is a long-term adventure but gives the best Returns on Investment (ROI). I hope this chapter has enlightened you on the basics of land banking I learned from Chief Razaq Okoya of Eleganza Groups of Companies.

CHAPTER 8
5 Land Banking Lessons from Alhaji Aliko Dangote

In this chapter, I want to buttress more on the wealth of mentorship by sharing the 5 land banking lessons I learnt from Alhaji Aliko Dangote (who happened to be a role model). While I look forward to meeting him in person, he has been a sustainable role model to me over the years. I admire his achievements and impact on society. One of the most powerful rules of well I have learnt is that *you do not attract what you despise.* Therefore, I learnt quickly never to despise people who are successful or seem to have gone ahead of me, mainly I desire to become like them. One of the things I often see as a paradox to me is how people want to be rich, but hate rich people, how people despise rich people and do name-calling even without facts about the people who are successful and claim all the ills about them. They accuse them of whatever it is they want to accuse them of, and I have learned not to do that.

I remember years ago, I used to struggle with that. Whenever I see a wealthy man with a big car, I'll say we don't know what they did; I see them as thieves. I do not speak that way again today because I've learned that not every rich person is a thief, and you will never attract what you despise. You will never become something that you look down on. If you look down on something, don't believe in something, or think something is wrong, you will never attract that and become that same person, which has taught me a lot.

Lesson One

I learned from Dangote that he does not buy cities. Dangote loves to buy bush. If I ask you today, which land do you prefer to buy, city or bush? You will tell me you want to buy a city, but do you know Dangote doesn't buy the city; he buys the bush? Check all of Dangote's properties; you know where he has most of his factories and refineries. They are not in the city; they're in the bush, and what many don't know is that most of those factories are massive real estate investments. Let me give you an example. One of them has a housing program of almost 500 houses for some of the staff. One of the factories I've seen they were able to build 500 houses, so if it's not real estate, tell me what it is. The last time I did a tour of the Dangote refinery that is currently under construction in Ibeju-Lekki, I saw a three-storey temporary shelter of over nine thousand (9,000) expatriates. These are temporary shelters, over nine thousand (9,000) for expatriates currently constructing the Dangote petroleum petrochemical refinery. Over 40,000 people are working in that refinery in Ibeju-Lekki right now, which is a massive level of investment. Dangote does not buy the city, and he buys the bush. The man is rich enough to have started a refinery in Banana Island, but he has not done that. He's rich enough to have started a refinery in Lekki Phase 1 and Phase 2; it will cost him much money, he has enough money to have done that, but you can't see him do that. Dangote does not buy cities, and he buys the bush.

The biggest lesson you want to learn from land banking is to buy bush because the bush of today is the latest city of tomorrow. Let me say that again, the bush of today is the latest city of tomorrow. Look at Cairo in Washington, Amazon has made Cairo the most expensive place for real estate in the world, technically because Cairo is the only place with the largest concentration of homeless people who have jobs, and that is because of Amazon.

Likewise, that is one of the biggest secrets people do not know about Ibeju-Lekki. Ibeju-Lekki is likely to become a city like that where people will have jobs but struggle to have a house because of the massive expansion and investment going on there, and that's what Dangote did. I want you to know where Dangote's refinery is in Ibeju Lekki. It's five times the size of Victoria Island.

This lesson I'm teaching will change your mindset for life, and you will learn how wealth is created, which is very important. Wealth is not what you need; it's ideas that create wealth. Ideas are what you need because once you have the ideas and understand them, you must act on them, and you're wealthy.

The biggest reason for poverty is not knowing what people do to be rich. Let me say that again, the most significant cause of poverty does not even know what to do to be rich. It's not the fact that you can't be wealthy; it's that you don't even know what to do to be rich; that is the biggest reason for failure and poverty. People fail not because there is no money to be made but because they do not know. Even the Bible talks about you not knowing the way to the city, not understanding the road that leads to the city. So, when people say to me, "I'm going to become rich, Dr Stephen", I say yes, "What you need is knowledge and execution of that knowledge. You need information on what wealthy people do and act on it."

One of my mentees is on his way to making his first 1 million dollars in his business, but the point is that, was that one million dollars not available five years ago? It was available. People made one million dollars five years ago, so what's changed? Quality information and willingness to execute it. When people talk about wealth and prosperity, it's not that you can't be wealthy; do you even know what to do? Do you even know what those who are wealthy are doing? Dangote does not buy the city but buys the bush. That's what he does: he buys the bush, and he buys them in bulk. That leads me to lesson two.

Lesson Two

Dangote does not buy small; instead, he buys bulk. The biggest mistake you can make when it comes to land banking is to buy little because years later, you will regret it. Back to the story of a man I helped sell land he bought for N12 million, N220 million 15 years later in Chapter 5; you will understand this lesson better.

When it comes to land banking, Dangote buys, in bulk acres. Can you imagine somebody buying five times the size of Victoria Island? He bought it one man, five times the size. The last time I was still on tour, I was told that Dangote was still looking for another massive acre, that the cooperative was looking to buy at least 50 acres to 100 acres, that they wanted to build housing for their staff, but they couldn't get it, the man buys bulk. When you want to invest in land banking, it's hard to buy bulk but try your best to buy bulk; it takes discipline, it takes sacrifice, it takes what we call delayed gratification, and the economics of scale and volume that's the rule right now.

One of the most legitimate ways to build wealth is through land banking. It's almost as if you have done a money ritual because the land that you bought for peanuts today is going to be very expensive tomorrow. So, Dangote buys bulk because he's aware a time may come; this refinery may have problems and challenges, and people may not even buy the product the refinery is producing again, but guess what? The entire community is already developed. So, if he decides to sell some part of that land, he would have raised more liquid which will have raised more money, and things will keep going on, and that's the power of doing volume when it comes to land banking.

Do bulk; 1 acre, 2 acres, 10 acres, particularly if you can partner with a credible real estate company like the one I run that can protect your estate or land for you till whatever time you are ready to develop it, which is what we do at Gtext Homes. And we're doing it well; when you buy property from Gtext Homes, you can go to sleep.

I remember a woman sent her brother because she had invested in the land before seeing it. She is not in Nigeria, just like most of our customers are not in the country; they invest out of trust. This woman got worried that she had to send her brother to go and check the land to be sure that the land truly existed. Her brother got there and gave her the good news, and she said, "I'm sorry; I want to apologise that I doubted you. I've just had too many experiences, family members had duped me when I bought land through them, so it was hard to believe that somebody I don't know from anywhere would sell land to me, and indeed, that land exists". I said, well, that's why we. Yoruba people will say, "If you close your eyes because you have seen too many evil people, you also close your eyes, and good people will pass, and you will miss them". If you want to be rich legitimately, all you need to know is how rich people are doing it. You need to know to study the lifestyle of rich people, their investment pattern, their attitude, and their pattern, and do things the same way they are doing it, and in a matter of time, you will get there.

Lesson Three

Alhaji Aliko Dangote focuses on areas with a high concentration of government projects to buy a parcel of land from there because of the Port Authority itself, and he built a factory there, and realised that there is a free trade zone in the Ibeju-Lekki. There are so many government projects on that axis that he bought. Always buy land where there is a concentration of government projects and infrastructure. I met people who said, "Dr Stephen, I started hearing this concept of land banking, and I bought land somewhere, and the land didn't appreciate". I said because you didn't learn where to invest. You see, half-knowledge is worse than ignorance. I've always said that you've learned so much from me doesn't mean you already know it, get mentorship. I always support people. My only request is to at least invest through my company before you start telling me to give you guidance on other forms of investment.

Lesson Four

Dangote always, and this is very important, increase the ROI (Return on Investment) of the places he buys land by over one thousand percent, and I'm going to tell you how and why. I'll give you an example of Ibeju-Lekki, where Dangote is right now, land used to go for 100,000 naira per plot or 50,000 naira per plot before Dangote got there. Today, to buy land without Government title in that same place, you are thinking of 2.5, 3, or 4 million naira and above. In that same place, to buy the one that has Government Excision or Gazette, you are looking at the range of 7 million naira, 10 million naira, 15 million naira, 20 million naira, some even sell more than 20 million. That is what the effect of Dangote has done in Ibeju-Lekki, and before Dangote got there, land was not that expensive. Even when there were plans that Lagos State Government would do a Free Trade Zone, the value of property did not increase until Dangote moved in.

I'll tell you a few things, and this is one of the lessons I've learned, Dangote always adds value to the land he acquires. He adds value by developing the land in factories that can employ one form or the other. So doing projects ultimately creates some form of employment, and migration makes all the difference.

When you do land banking, find some value you can add to the land. For example, you can start a farm on the land, a school, a hospital etc. Just find a way to do something such that your presence increases the value of that land. Right now, in Jasper Estate. We have started fencing and adding value to the land, so it keeps appreciating. So, the land that used to go for X amount before you know its, value has appreciated.

Lesson Five

Dangote always buys land close to a water source. He bought land in Apapa, and you could see that massive investment close to the water. See the one he did at Ibeju-Lekki, close to the water. I can go on and on and show you several projects that Dangote has done he's never afraid of buying places close to the sea.

Rich people like water areas. That is why there's Victoria Island surrounded by water. There is a Banana Island, the wealthiest island, the most expensive land in the world. There is Lekki, and what people don't know about Lekki is that on the right-hand side of Lekki is the Atlantic Ocean and the left-hand side of Lekki is the Lagoon. Many people think Ibeju-Lekki is a coincidence, but it's not. Ibeju-Lekki is the replication of Lekki; that's why the unique thing about Ibeju-Lekki is that it is the same model as Lekki Phase 1 and Lekki Phase 2 in Lagos State.

Land with water always appreciates more than dry land. So when Lekki started developing, people kept warning others not to buy Lekki, that the water would carry them away. But for whatever reason, the middle and higher class bought because they just liked water areas, and kept staying there.

Dangote will most likely be one of the richest persons in the world once the Ibeju-Lekki refinery is launched, because the kind of money he will be making every day from that refinery to be crazy. It is the most significant single-line refinery in the world. The entire investment costs a whopping 16 billion dollars. It is a whole lot, but the man is doing it.

These are many lessons, and like I said, I took time to share these with you in this book because many people don't know that you do not attract what you resist. You do not attract what you hate. If you despise something, you don't attract it. If you hate rich people, you can't be rich. It is not a curse; it's just how it works. So, you have to be willing to learn from them because you need to learn what they are doing if you want to replicate them. Success is replicable, but you have to know what people are doing that has made them wealthy and how you can do the same. You need to know the processes and principles and how to execute the same principle. That is how wealth is created, how you become rich, and if you can do what you are reading from this book, which I have also learned from Dangote, you too can become wealthy.

PART THREE
PREFERENCE: LAND VERSUS HOUSE?

CHAPTER 9
The 5 Benefits of Land Banking Investment

"If you ask for common advice, you'll get common results. If you ask for extraordinary advice, you will get extraordinary results."

–Dr. Stephen Akintayo

Let me introduce our company–Gtext Holdings. We are a Digital Marketing, Real Estate and Consulting firm. We started 14 years ago, particularly in digital marketing, and we've grown over the years. Seven years ago, we diversified into real estate, and it's been an incredible journey. We are one of Africa's fastest growing real estate companies.

Gtext Homes Vision:

Our vision is to be the world's largest developer of Green and Smart Homes.

How we run with this vision explains how we solve some of these challenges directly or by partnering with people. We have agencies we partner with people–for folks who have land or have houses; we help them sell. We meet every real estate need because we have a goal of 100 million housing problems sorted out.

Gtext Homes Mission:

Our vision is to be the largest developer of Green and Smart Homes in the world using innovation and technology.

Real estate investment involves purchasing, managing, managing, and selling land for profits by individuals and organisations. Also, one of the beauties of real estate in Nigeria is that it yields up to a minimum of 500% returns in five years if you choose a good location. It's only in Nigeria and Africa that you can get this. That is quite impossible, even in some developed countries. Many people have shared testimonies of how they invested in property, and the property grew and multiplied.

Let's move on to more benefits of land banking. I'll share 5 with you in this book.

The first one is that you can always determine the price of your land. In other words, when it comes to land, the evaluation and pricing mechanisms are more flexible. However, it is not easy. Let's assume you spent N50 million to build a house and proceeded to sell it for N100 million; it's tough because the evaluators will evaluate it and tell you this house is probably worth less than N50 million and as well consider the diminishing returns, maintenance, etc. You have to know that the gap of making a considerable profit is very rare. Only in land investment can you make up to 500% returns, when you buy land in a unique place, voila! Great returns!

Let me give you an example; in places like Opebi and Lekki Phase One in Lagos State, when you have a house, and want to sell it, usually more value is placed on the land than the house. That is because, in most cases, the person who can afford to buy that house probably even wants something better. E.g., his taste when it comes to designs and stuff like that might be higher and better, and in most cases may want to demolish it and then build to his taste.

The second benefit of buying land compared to a house for real estate investment is that the ability for land to have potential development opportunities is higher. This means that there is flexibility on the buyer's part, and that's why it's a lot better when you're buying land than a house. Here's an example: many times, when people buy a particular place, they buy for the land, not the house. In most cases, people–the buyer–want to demolish it. That can cost the buyer more money and have them discouraged. This is because the buyer also wants to invest. For example, we have some places where a bank wants to situate their bank there, and they prefer an empty land because there's a different structure in terms of how they will build their banking hall or a situation with the telecommunication mast. If somebody has a property somewhere and that's a good location to situate the mast in terms of telecommunication, if there is a house in that particular place, they have to demolish it and put the mast there, which is an extra cost. But if you invest in empty land, you can make it flexible for the buyer to buy from you.

The third benefit of land banking is unique. It is that it's cheaper for you to buy, so you can acquire more. For example, if you're buying land that is a lot cheaper and you can buy in large quantities.

Please note that you don't just buy land. Not all lands are worth purchasing. There are certain things to look out for before you purchase land. One of them, for example, is knowing the future development plan in that location. Another is answering the question, does the land have water? That is because only rich people buy land and houses where there's water. Poor people don't know because of the ill economic mindset. More reason why all the most sought-after places in Lagos are waterlogged. This is likewise synonymous with Florida in America. Its uniqueness is water, and this is why it is one of the most sought-after and best places all over the world. Florida is full of lakes.

Now, here is a mighty secret. Did you know that the foods of champions are challenges? Meanwhile, the food of the poor is an excuse and more excuses.

The fourth benefit of investing in land versus a house is that it is much easier to sell land than a house. When it comes to investment, you will often decide whether you want to dispose of your investment perhaps to raise more money for another attractive investment or another purpose. It is a lot harder to sell a house compared to land. Building true wealth is not about how much you're making but about how much you are saving and investing. If it's a house you have tied your money down with, it's a lot difficult to dispose of the house eventually but it's much easier to dispose of land.

And the last benefit of buying land for investment versus buying a house is that its maintenance cost is zero naira–absolutely nothing! However, it costs much money to maintain a house. E.g., the painting and repairs. Else, one day, God forbid something happened to the house, and it went down. So buying land is a lot smarter than a house when it comes to real estate investment, particularly when you're investing for the long run.

For land encroachment, one of the best things you can do to prevent it is to buy into an estate. Estate owners and developers always protect the whole land whether you have bought it. Peradventure, you bought it from *omo onile,* and you didn't buy from an estate, you can decide to lease it out to farmers and to some people, but make sure you have substantial agreements with them and make sure you are spiritually vibrant so that they don't attack you when you want to come for your land. However, in most cases, I always tell people the best option is to buy from a company. Even if there's an issue, in the case of debt, the company is a living entity on its own, and you can always go ahead and get what you want.

Mentorship in Land banking

Now I will touch a bit on mentorship. Regardless of your ambition, you need a mentor to succeed and make fewer mistakes. Someone once said, "A fool learns from his mistakes, while the wise learn from other people's mistakes". Ask questions from those who have gone ahead of you. Enquire from them what they wish they did right or better. Ask questions about their early days in business and the structure they adopt in navigating challenging moments. Seek mentorship. It is of paramount importance, and you cannot talk it away. I have coaches, and after talking to them, I am much more enlightened and directed on what to do and not do. I mentor and coach people as well. However, we can discuss more on this over the course of this book, should you need mentorship. I can easily access any of my social media platforms, and the handle is Stephen Akintayo. A mentor can even guide you against purchasing the wrong land because they know the history of that land. There are numerous benefits to being coached by a professional/expert in your field. Contact me today at +971588283572 or +234818000618 for mentorship.

CHAPTER 10
Why Land Banking is Better Than Buying A House for Nigerians in Diaspora

"If you don't find a way to make money while you sleep, you will work until you die."

-Warren Buffett

Why do you want to buy a house? There are 2 reasons. One is returning to Nigeria to live there or to be able to live there whenever you're in Nigeria. Another is buying a house to rent it out. Now, the majority of Nigerians in the diaspora don't visit Nigeria often.

There's this issue of consistency in the Nigerian context. For example, if you run a company in Nigeria and somebody steals from you, and then you sack that person, folks will begin to plead for forgiveness on the person's behalf. That can only happen in Nigeria. It's only in Nigeria that your tenant doesn't pay your rent, and other people will call you a wicked landlord for asking your tenant to leave. You need to know the realities here; everything is emotional, psychological, sentimental, and what have you in Nigeria. So I laugh when Nigerians in the diaspora say, "I want to buy a house so that I can rent it out and make money". I laugh because that isn't always a tangible option except in specific locations in Nigeria. For example, if you have your house in Banana Island, the calibre of persons that would even rent a house in Banana Island wouldn't want issues, so they will pay your rent. If your house is in Ikoyi, any individual who rents it will have his/her reputation to protect. As such, your rent will be paid. But you are buying a house in Badagry, Abule Egba, Sango or Ibadan, and you think your tenants will be faithful with the rent; I must let you know that you're deceiving yourself, particularly since you're not even in Nigeria.

So, I've had experiences, and one is with a young man who, before he left for Baltimore about 5 years ago, bought this house in Nigeria for 25 million naira or thereabout, and then he left. Unfortunately, he couldn't get a single person to rent it for 3 years. Then I told him, "If you had bought land with that 25 million naira, I know you cannot resell it in five years. Now, that's on a conservative level. On a non-conservative level, you will sell that same land for 200 million naira".

Many tend to miss what I'm about to share. So, in reality, when you buy the house as a diasporan, you struggle to get tenants to rent the house or you even get tenants but are not paying your rent. However, it's not just that; the second is that when you buy a house, you will still need to be the one carrying out some major maintenance on that property; many times, the tenants will still have to get back to you on issues relating to the repair or purchase of a new pumping machine. It's not like the tenant is going to pay for a new pumping machine; I hope you know that. Certain major requirements still demand your attention and intervention even while in the diaspora. The ultimate concept of wealth creation is investing in something that you can go to bed, and while you're asleep, it is appreciating. That is what land banking does. When you invest in land banking, what it does is that it has a way of helping you build wealth without adding more money. But in a case where building a house is involved, you will still need to keep up with regular maintenance payments, and this is inconsequential. Whether your tenant is paying your rent or not, necessity is laid upon you to pay specific major bills and as well take care of certain significant things in that house.

So, for you in the diaspora, owning a house in Nigeria might not be the best option. However, it's a good option if you have people to help you manage it. If you can afford to build a house in certain highbrow places, it will be of great advantage for you and particularly areas where you can use it for Air BnB and short lease; this is one of the investment opportunities you venture into, with my focus on Nigerians in the diaspora.

Let me divert my attention to those of us who cannot afford price rates between 75 to 200 million naira for house purchase to buy a house in the kind of environment where the calibre of people who rent those kinds of houses stay. Some of them it's a company that rents the house for their staff, and the company pays you directly. At the same time, some of them are well-to-do. Some even have their property; it may not just be in that location. So they will not owe you rent, but in certain areas where you can build your house, and you can be guaranteed that they will owe you rent. I must emphatically tell you this because people will use sentiments such as 'I lost my job', 'Oh, Coronavirus, they didn't pay us in our place of work', 'God will bless you', 'Uncle, Oga, na God I beg you.' Meanwhile, you look back 5 years down the line; they owe you, you've spent much money to build a house, and you are not making money from it. In some cases, what you want is not bad, but it may not be the best idea or concept because you are not on the ground.

However, the question is, what, then, is the problem with buying land in Nigeria as a Nigerian in the diaspora? Of course, if you buy land in Nigeria, the question is, who will help you protect your land? We all know that *omo onile* can sell one piece of land to five or even ten people. I mean the land they give to you; one day, you will get there, and somebody else has built on it. We all know that problem exists, and that's a reality. And that's why many diasporans prefer a house because they usually think, 'If I build a house, nobody's just going to take over my house. It is my house, and it's there. But if it's land, you will wake up one day to find that it has been sold to somebody else, some other people have taken over the property, and I'm wondering what's going on?' That is true. It happens a lot of the time. It even happened to me, though.

I partnered with my brother to build a house for my father in

Abeokuta. I couldn't go, so I just released my portion of the money, and to my amazement, they kept reselling this land to different people again and again. I had to personally go there and look for who the most notorious of the *omo onile* is. I got the person on my side, and that was how the challenge capsized. While the reality is that things like this happen, the solution ultimately is to look for credible real estate companies. Before you say that real estate companies are more expensive than buying directly from *omo onile,* that's true. But you don't know that they've also factored in what I call PR money. In Nigeria, there is undoubtedly a kind of money we call PR money, or you can call it Public Relations money. Politicians call it security votes. In business, we call it PR money.

That is why I always advise people to buy land from real estate companies to make sure that your land, property, investment, etc., is secure, and any day and any time, you can hold the real estate companies responsible till you eventually take over your property. Thus, I often laugh when people complain that real estate companies are expensive and give high bids because many don't even understand or know that they do not own the land they are buying from *omo onile.* They will sell it to five people, and you fight yourselves. Aside from that, sometimes, they will sell it to you and later, some other people will come back to claim that it was two families that sold it to you while they are 5 families. Dragging this back and forth will lead to litigation. Events like these occur, but real estate companies have a way of having a grip on these people, and it has always helped. So, you don't know that you are protecting your investment when you say, "I am buying my land from a real estate company." Because once you pay the real estate company and they are credible, by the way, you need to do your research on the company you want to deal with; you can rely on them to ensure that your investment is secured and intact. However, I want to also advise you that when buying property from a real estate company, always ensure you do it right.

For some of us, if you are going to be a wealthy person from real estate investment, you have to be humble. Humility is vital if you're going to become wealthy regarding real estate investment. One of the biggest challenges Nigerians in the diaspora have is a lack of humility. I'm aware that you live in the U.K. or in Canada where there are possessions of excellent basic social amenities like good roads and electricity with every other thing well structured. I am also aware that if you are to buy a house $500,000 today, you may not need to deposit more than 10 to $20,000 initial payments, and then maybe in the next six months, you will pay another $50,000. I know that's how it works, and yet it's going to be a five-bedroom duplex with your garage and maximum electricity. Everything seems perfect. But it's not that easy! You need to wake up! You don't just get a property that way. First, the flexible payment is not as simple and easy as it is in developed countries. We will get there. Nigeria will also get there. We believe strongly that the banking sector will support real estate companies more over time; the government will support more always to give real estate companies C of Os and things like that so that banks can support them. We will get there, but we are not there yet. So sometimes, the place you want is Lekki Phase one because that connects with the calibre of place you live in now. But life is in phases, and men are in sizes; live your size at a time. If you cannot afford Lekki Phase one, if all you can afford is Lagos-Ibadan express road, buy it. Buy it if you can afford it in Ibadan, Atan-Ota, Mushin Olosha, Shangisha or Ibafo. Life is in phases, and men are in sizes, so live your size per time.

One of the biggest problems we face as Africans (Nigerians) in the Diaspora is that we prefer to consume rather than produce. The bitter truth is that these countries you enjoy and love were not that way years ago. It was our cocoa money that was used to develop the U.S. and London; perhaps you never knew. It was our petroleum product (our crude oil) that they stole from us before independence that they used to do those things. Wake up and smell the coffee! It was the gold they were illegally mining from Africa that they used to develop those countries you admire now. It wasn't just your tax. Your tax was used to maintain it and not to build it. We need to face reality here. Those beautiful countries you live in used to be like this many years ago.

John D. Rockefeller was the man who made the breakthrough in the petroleum sector in America. You can confirm with the use of Google. Andrew Carnegie was the brain behind the rail system in America, as well as the steel system in America. He was a private citizen. One man developed the entire rail and steel sector in America. It wasn't the government. J.P. Morgan, a private company, was the person who developed the banking sector that we are using globally today! These countries did not develop overnight, and it took years. It took a fight; It took a whole lot to get to where it is today! If we develop Africa, we also need to be patient.

Did you know that as of 1990, Dubai was still sand? The place called Sheikh Zayed Road had barely 5 buildings. Yes, that same Dubai, you know. It took time and years of investment from all over the world with legal and illegal money to build the Dubai you see today. Good things take time. So, dear Nigerians in the diaspora, you need to be patient and understand that cultures and issues are different. I remember that we bought a particular land, and after we paid the family all that needed to be done, the community's youths sent us a letter saying that we should pay them 25 million naira. This happened for real. I remember that we even went to the police station of that region, and what the police officers could do was advise us to find a way to negotiate with the youths and move on. That is the reality of the system that we work in Nigeria. I strongly advise you to be humble and start at a phase at the level you can afford. Ultimately, you will build wealth if you are consistent.

Let me share my story with you. Our first sets of properties were where you couldn't even access the place. I remember one of the first lands I sold; I was the agent. The day they were taking me to the land, if not that company's MD/CEO and my biological elder brother started the company together, I would have doubted where we were going. I'm not kidding you. The reason is that we veered off the road, and kept going for almost an hour before getting to this place. Now, the funny thing about the land is that as at then in 2012, the land was worth 500,000 naira. It was in Shimawa, Lagos State, extremely bushy. Today, if you want to buy that same land, you can't get that land if you do not have five million - ten million naira. As of then, I was a broker, just marketing for other real estate companies.

I didn't have my own company. Today the place is fenced with people now living there. Incidentally, it's far from the new Redeemed Christian Church of God (RCCG) camp auditorium. It's gone now. Patience paid off. Folks who had the money in 2012 and refused to purchase the land with the far distance as an excuse even when they had the money no longer have 500,000 naira and didn't invest it either. The money didn't appreciate. That is very important regarding investment, especially for those of us in the diaspora.

Please note you should invest in land banking than in a house. The number one reason is that when you buy a house, you will struggle to get people to rent it. Number two, you struggle to get Nigerians to pay house rent even when people rent it.

Number three, your colleagues who have houses in places I told you are probably places with better tenancy payments. If you have a house in Ikoyi, don't worry; most likely, your tenants will pay you well and upfront. If you have a house in Lekki Phase one, your tenant will most likely pay you because of the calibre of people living there. If you have a house in Magodo or Omole, it's almost 50/50, but there's a good chance of being paid in those places. But you will find it difficult to get your rent for other areas outside that.

Number four is that you still need to keep spending money to maintain the house, except you want the house to become a shamble totally. You will still need to spend money regularly to maintain the property, from the pumping machine to the metallic damage of the gate. But if you do land banking, you already know you're not touching that land until the next five-ten years. As such, you know that you will have gotten at least a hundred percent return on investment in five to ten years. Imagine a land you bought for 10 million would have appreciated to about 20 to 50 million. That is how it works! With this approach, you will not need to spend more money on maintenance. You just watch your land appreciates. Thus, I always advise people to **do land banking.** But when you're doing land banking, don't buy from *omo onile*. Instead, look for a credible company to buy from. Now to the questions mostly asked:

1. How can one guarantee that this land is safe?

The guarantee is to make sure you buy from a credible real estate company. That's step 1. Step 2 is to ensure that the owners of the real estate company you buy from have online and public appearances. Please note that for anybody who puts their faces out on social media, if they are not real, people will come for them at some point. Per adventure, there's a dispute with such individuals; they will be easily located because of their feasible appearance. However, the challenge is that many of us put our money in companies where we don't even know the owner, and the company is not feasible. When you buy from a real estate company, it is the job of the real estate company to safeguard your land. For example, for as many who bought from all our estates, it is our job and responsibility to make sure their land is and remains safe. The advantage of buying from a company is that it is the job of the real estate company you paid money to preserve and safeguard your land, even the day you start building, as long as you inform them, whatever they need to do to make sure that construction goes smoothly, they will do. They know the people they bought the land from and do PR for. The company and the landowner become almost like a family, so you can hold the company accountable for the safety of your land. While buying from a company is always costly, buying directly is penny-wise pound foolish. Which would you prefer? Purchasing the land that has already been sold to like 4 other people for 1 million naira only to combat police mitigation while spending more money on a lost case? Or buying that same property for 2 million naira with a full guarantee of safety from a credible real estate company like Gtext Homes, and watching your land appreciate in multiple folds as the years progress?

2. Is there a need to always fence the land you buy?

There is a need if you are buying it from *omo onile* because if you don't fence your land at a significant height, put a big gate, and lock the place, you don't have land. I did this for the lands I bought for my family members as a gift in the state where I came from. But if you don't want to be involved in unnecessary stress, approach a credible real estate company for your land purchase. You won't need to fence your land because, ultimately, the real estate company will first do perimeter fencing, and even if they didn't fence it, they would protect the entire land.

3. How can someone get natural land?

To begin with, work with a legitimate,,, credible company that is on the ground in Nigeria. In addition, learn about land titles and the implication of those titles, at least a basic knowledge. For example, know terms like Survey, C of O, land lease, etc. Ignorance of land matters is too much, and that's why there is so much fear and distrust.

I remember a lady chatting with me one day. She paid for a house with a company I know. She paid them N20 million out of N25 million but has not gotten her house. Based on my finesse in real estate, I asked some questions, and she gave the correct answers. By the time she was done explaining, I had counselled her on what to do, and everything worked out well, though she never bought from our company. The thing is, you don't need to pull others down to make ahead moves. There's a law of sowing and reaping, and it is legit.

Please note that to process your C of O, you can't spend less than three million naira, even if you already have the land and already pay the family for the land. Therefore, be suspicious of any land selling at a lesser price with an expectation of it having C of O. Anybody selling land to you in Lagos and claiming that the land has C of O and the land is less than six million, is lying to you. I am referring to Epe, Ibeju-Lekki, Badagry, Ikorodu, and so on. **The more the title, the more expensive the property is.** The price can range from ten to fifty million naira because they have C of Os. Thus, we need to educate people to understand land document titles.

PART FOUR
NON-NEGOTIABLE VIRTUES FOR LAND BANKERS

CHAPTER 11
Investment Disciplines For Transgenerational Wealth in Land Banking

In this chapter, we will discuss the various disciplines in land banking investments that would guarantee transgenerational wealth in your life and your family.

Where do we begin?

"Discipline", according to Merriam-Webster Dictionary, can be defined as "an orderly or prescribed conduct or pattern of behaviour, a rule or system of rules governing conduct or activity."

Wikipedia says, "Generational wealth refers to financial assets passed by one generation of a family to another. Those assets include cash, stocks, bonds and other investments, as well as real estate and family businesses".

Based on the above definitions, we can safely say that *land banking investment disciplines for transgenerational wealth are those prescribed conduct, the pattern of behaviour, rule or system of rules in land banking that result in wealth and fortune for oneself and future generations.*

The following are disciplines that guarantee transgenerational wealth in one's life:

Discipline One
Take more land banking risk despite previous losses, but this time, get a mentor.

"The biggest risk is not taking any risk. In a world that is changing quickly, the only strategy guaranteed to fail is not taking any risk"- Mark Zuckerberg.

I have made over a billion naira in land banking, and have also had my share of losses. However, the last loss I encountered in land banking was one hundred and twenty million naira (N120 million). I would not be here today if I decided to give up when I lost one hundred and twenty million naira.

"Wealth is a reward for the risk you took. If you don't take the risk, you can kiss wealth and riches goodbye because it can't happen without it! Wealthy people are risk-takers; they take the risk."

I have discovered the most competent people are poor people. It takes much smartness to be poor. I say this because poor people are so bright in analysing *that they end up paralysis (anaemic financial acumen and portfolio).* The acronym for the word poor is; PASSING OVER OPPORTUNITIES REPEATEDLY because of the fear of not taking the risk. One of the greatest secrets of my life is that I never announce my losses until I've recovered from them; if not, many people would come up with all the beautiful reasons not to do business or investment, and that would have discouraged me, I see this happening in Africa, the pity party that Africans do only make us poorer. In order not to continually repeat the same mistakes, GET A MENTOR!

In retrospect, not just someone you like but a person who has proven expertise and results in the area you desire to be mentored. That's who a mentor is; where else to look for if not me? Yes, me! I'm qualified to mentor you because the success I have acquired in real estate in just a short time (7 years) is impressive! Twenty estates for that limited number of time, incredible! With all humility, I'd be delighted to show you the way, too, as I've helped many people achieve financial freedom through land banking. Poor people always listen to people who are like them or worse than them. One of the significant differences between the rich and the poor is that while poor people listen and follow their kind, the rich only listens to people more extensive than they are; when a rich person sees another richer than himself, he will do one of two things, either opt for friendship, or mentorship considering the age difference, the reverse remains the case when poor people come in the presence of rich people, they either castigate, envy, despise or criticise them rather than try to learn the secrets and principles they deployed to be entrusted with great wealth, it's the same energy beloved! It's the same energy! The energy to learn from rich people is the same energy you use to criticise them; the latter would never benefit you because you can never attract what you despise; the former is always a better option, your choice.

For instance, the rumour went on about the lavish money spent at Obi Cubana's mother's funeral (the video went viral) and had a lot of attention and views on social media. I didn't join the naysayers and critics. Instead, I resorted to learning the source of his wealth and great fortune. I discovered that he is a legitimate businessman; he owns luxurious clubs in Lagos and Abuja, far finer than his house at Oba, Anambra State.

At the time he buried his mother, he built several hotels and resorts to lodge his billionaire friends across the nation who came for the burial, thus making money during the period; I also noticed, he didn't spray money. It was his friends that sprayed the money and everything that happened during the event was more like a marketing tool and strategy to launch further and propel his businesses.

You may think wealthy people are wasteful, and they spend much money on costly items; that may be true, but only half of the truth, the reason being *it takes money to make money.*

For instance, if I have a client willing to invest N100 - N200 million naira in Gtext's Green and Smart homes. What car would convince him more to do business with me; a Rolls Royce or a Toyota Corolla? I believe the answer is clear, and the same goes for a private jet or any other luxurious item you think rich people have; it's all a marketing tool that helps us progress in our business. I never castigate anyone; rather, I learn from them and apply relevant principles to my life and business.

There is no traffic at the top; all you need to do is to learn the same principles and then pay the price. What a lazy man calls luck is reality because opportunity has met preparation.

Discipline Two
Add value to the land.

After you have purchased a strategic place for land banking, endeavour to add value to the land or only buy lands that they are adding value to, even if that value is not done by you, a land that has the potential to appreciate so much in value due to the various development projects in that particular location and its surroundings. Speaking of "adding value," according to Goldman Sachs records, the areas that have the highest return on investment in Africa (in decreasing order) are;

1. Lagos.
2. Abuja.
3. Port Harcourt
4. South Africa.

It's the scale of preference for me. Do your research. Wisdom demands that you start investing in the places that have the most significant returns on your money before other areas, including your village; building an apartment in your home town is a beautiful thing to do. However, it will interfere with your wealth creation, two people drowning are useless to each other, it takes the freedom of one to help the other. Be wealthy first, accumulate every fortune you possibly can, then out of your abundance, go home and help your village people if that is your desire.

Some of these projects that can add value to the land include but are not limited to the following:

1. Fence the land round.
2. Do the internal road of that land.
3. Do specific projects like golf courses, polo clubs, and tennis courts.

4. Plant trees.

5. Build resorts and hotels around the estate or location; all these add value to the land.

Another example is Nicon Estate, Lekki Phase 2. Other lands in that area did not appreciate as much as Nicon Estate; why is that? Because those who bought the Nicon estate did many development projects. The infrastructure, drainage, and estate were well done and attracted wealthy people to buy, and build there, so the value appreciated faster than in other places.

Bonny Island, located in Port Harcourt, Nigeria, was built by NLNG (Nigeria Liquefied Natural Gas), an oil and gas producing company looks different from every other place; it's like a different world entirely in terms of electricity and infrastructure because the owners took the time, and effort resources to develop the land. Did you know the surroundings of Bonny Island are more expensive than the city centres in Port Harcourt because of the value?

When doing land banking, ask yourself, "These people I'm buying land from, are they futuristic? Do they have plans?" We at Gtext Homes are not just doing any estate but service plots for people who think like Elon Musk and are futuristic. A portion of our estates would have a place to charge electric cars, and we are recycling every energy and not connecting to PHCN (Power Holding Company of Nigeria). We are our PHCN! Buying land in such locations is how you build wealth, not by chance or mistake. Most times why people lose money because they are emotional and sentimental rather than rational; they trust their relatives instead of credible agents or property brokers who have good reviews. If a company has lasted at least five years, it will show in its reviews online. For those in the diaspora, seven out of ten people were duped, and swindled by family members, while others did not do thorough research before investing. Wake up! In Gtext Homes, our integrity is impeccable, you don't need a third party, but you can get one if that's what you want; we would send you documents of our agreement anywhere in the world, even if it's Afghanistan.

Discipline Three
Start with what you can afford.

You can always start at your level. A wise man said, "A journey of a thousand miles begins with a step" so crucial! When we first started, our land was waterlogged, but that's all I had at the time; I didn't despise it. I used what the Almighty provided, damning the consequences. If I had not taken that little step, without waiting for things to get favourable, I wonder where I'd be by now, back then we were begging them to invest in the estate with just N750,000; right now, if you don't have N8, 000,000 you can't afford it. Gtext Homes has acquired 20 estates in just seven years, talk of exploits! That, right there, is the power of small beginnings.

The Bible says, "Despise not the day of little beginnings", true! Utilise every opportunity to start small; it's okay to start where you are but don't remain there. It's a mystery, but I have discovered, every time you invest money wisely, supernaturally, you get more money; every time you invest in real estate, you get more real estate. The only possible explanation I can muster is that when the Almighty created man, the first assignment He gave him was to acquire real estate, And Elohim blessed them, *"Bear fruit and increase, and fill the earth and subdue it, and rule over the fish of the sea, and the birds of the heaven, and all creatures moving on the earth"- Gen. 1:28.*
The Mighty One commanded man to dominate and subdue the earth, not one another, the word "subdue" can invariably mean to "acquire more land, acquire more property".

Discipline Four
As you acquire enough land banking, switch to rental income.

Sell one plot, then use the money to build a rental income; this is why you must buy more than one plot. At least three plots of land or an acre would be enough for a start, such that when you've sold and made money from one plot, you can use the money to develop the other plots. Don't just buy land because you want to live there; the primary goal of buying land is to sell it and generate cash flow; that's how it is done!

I will share with you life lessons of how this occurred in my students and people I know; the first story is;

Just 500 naira
While I taught in London on this subject, there was an old retiree, a woman of age seventy-two who at one time lived in Nigeria and worked as a Headteacher, I hear her story; "I remember at my place of work back then (Isale Eko) people used to bring A4 paper with columns of instalment payment depending on what you can afford, to buy land at Admiralty, Lekki Phase 1. My juniors used to rush and pay for it and when they came to me, I baulked; saying, "Nigeria is not working, I want to go to London, I want to work in London". Then I'd go ahead and turn down the offer; I was too arrogant to see the amazing opportunity that was presented to me at the time, plus, I wasn't interested; all my focus was to go to London. Little did I know, I missed an opportunity of a lifetime. Some opportunities come just once in your life; if you miss them, you've missed them! And so I did, a chance that would have made me financially free all my life. What's too sad about the whole story is that, after being retired from civil service, I still work in foster care to take care of myself, seeing my children have other responsibilities, and the little money they give me is not enough. While I appreciate the Highest that my children schooled abroad, those 'juniors' are now owners of homes worth billions of naira in Admiralty. Their rent alone is enough to afford their trip to and from London, and guess where they lodge when they come here? In a five-star hotel in this same London. What amazing lives they lead, and I'm still very much dependent on the meagre salary that comes from this foster care job. The

last time I tried to buy a property at Abule Egba, Lagos, for I still love Nigeria I would love to come back home; they said it was worth fifteen million naira. Where on earth would I be able to raise such an amount of money from this foster care? No! It's not possible. That is my story; all young people heed his teaching; he's telling the truth" she beckons to the audience to listen to the truth I was teaching on land banking and the enormous benefits accrued to you when you invest.

My take on this is that nothing stopped her from still going to London; all she had to do was pay a small amount of 300,500 naira, and the rest is history. I held my head, alarmed at such regret and loss. Don't let this be you; make hay while the sun shines, invest while you still can, when you still can, with whatever you can, before it's too late.

From 25 million to 3 billion naira
Haven learned the principle of land banking from His father, Pastor Paul Adefarasin, Founder and President of House on the Rock Church worldwide, applied the same knowledge to his life and got the same results. Being a Pastor at Victoria Island, Lagos, he desired ten acres of land, but the lands in his current location were too expensive, and he couldn't afford it; all they had as a ministry for the project at hand was just 25 million naira. So what he did was look for land on the outskirts of the city; he bought the land at Lagos end (Oriental Hotels) and left it for 10 years. A survey was done to ascertain the value of the land; that land is worth 3 billion naira as I write to you. It is currently the location of the headquarters of his successful ministry. Glory!

CHAPTER 12

HOW I STARTED MY MULTI-BILLION NAIRA LAND BANKING EMPIRE WITHOUT CASH I

By experience, I have discovered that the best places to buy land are near major cities, which include: Lagos, Abuja, Dubai, etc.

According to Lee J. Colan, "All great things started as one small thing".

I once started a business with just N1,000. As of then, it was ten dollars, and our real estate empire started seven years ago. I started without capital or cash.

A common complaint among potential entrepreneurs is the lack of capital. In this chapter, I'm going to prove that you already have all you need to start a land banking empire; you don't need capital. Everything you need is already available within your reach. Read on to find out how I built my multi-billion dollar land banking empire in 7 years without cash so that you can build yours too.

YOUR MONEY IS ON YOUR TONGUE

2015 was a remarkable one for me in the history of my existence. That is because that was when I ventured into the real estate business. However, before I started my real estate journey, I had always been a Digital Marketer.

It happened that a real estate company booked an appointment to see me. The founder of this company came to me and said he wanted to learn how to use the internet to sell his real estate business. He paid me for one week of training, and I remember that I told him and his team about how I have a lot of big dreams during the training. I also mentioned that one of the businesses I believe I'm going to do very soon is **real estate,** and I'm going to do it in a big way.

Little did I know that my help was in that room. I want you to write this down and keep it somewhere you can always see it "My money is on my tongue". Many of us do not know we have misused our tongues, which is why many of us are poor. Your money is on your tongue. If I did not mention that day that I intended to build a massive real estate empire, I would have missed that opportunity to break into real estate. After the training, the same man who said he had a problem walked up to me and said, "I heard you say you want to go into real estate." I replied affirmatively, "I desire to, but I don't have the money. I believe I'm going to have a big real estate company."

He smiled and said, "I have 250 acres of land that I am struggling to sell, which is why I came to you. Can I give you 50 acres of land to sell? I know you're a man of integrity. So as you make sales, you can pay me back." That was the beginning of my breakthrough story in the real estate industry!

Your money is on your tongue! If I did not say it that day that I intended to do real estate, even though I didn't have the money, I would not be here today, and we would not have built a multi-billion naira corporation. So, I want to beg you to start using your tongue correctly. I know things are tough. I know you may not have money, but don't say that. Instead, speak prosperity, speak abundance, speak increase, speak what you want to see, not what you don't want.

Let me ask you a question: Do you dress up when you get to where you are going, or walk naked to where you are going?

OK, I suppose your answer to both questions is No.

Do you dress up before you get where you're going the way you want to look?

Great, I guess your answer is a Yes!

In the same way, you must use your tongue because you don't wait to get to a place to dress the way you should look. So, for example, when you're going for a job interview, you don't wait till you get to the place of the job interview before you dress for the job.

Many of you wear your suit on time because you're going for a job interview.

Did the interview start at your house? No, but you dress in your house ahead of a job interview. So henceforth, you're going to let your tongue speak about your future and not your today. So let me say that again, and I want you to write this down, "Let your tongue speak about where you are going and not where you are".

MY SECRET IN BUILDING A MULTI-BILLION NAIRA REAL ESTATE BUSINESS REVEALED

My story of building a multi-billion naira real estate business is beyond inspirational. I have received so much favour in the sight of God and men. So many factors led to my success in the real estate industry, but I will share my top secrets with you because I want you to be the next billionaire Land Banker, and I guarantee that if you practise it, you will surely see results.

1. Become a Property Broker

My number 1 secret is that I first became a property broker. I had been selling property as a broker before I met the man that offered to give me 50 acres of land, but technically that's what I did because his giving me 50 acres of land means he still owns the land until I pay him before I become the owner. Being a broker is the first tool used to start a real estate business without money. You can start as a broker, sell for other people, get a good commission, and make money.

If you're an intelligent investor, you don't waste money anyhow; you begin to build your money gradually.

In most cases, if you're outstanding over time, people will see that you're good at selling; they may decide to give you 5 acres of land to sell at whatever price but tell you the price they want to collect from you when you sell, maybe between $2,500 - $5,000 from you per plot. You can sell at whatever price and pay them what they request. Note that before you can be trusted like this, you must have proven to be a person of integrity. If you don't build integrity, you can't go far in business. Integrity is key. You can cheat one or two people and think you are smart, but it's going to catch up with you, so for you to be a successful broker, you must have integrity.

For instance, people wired money to us in Dubai to help them buy properties. The money ranged from 250,000 - 1,000,000 dollars, and some even paid to our company's account, not even to the Developer, but the integrity to make sure we got their property for them was there. We did not mix their money with our money, and that is why we have a good name today. So people used to tell themselves, "If he's Dr Stephen, go and sleep, your money is safe with him".

That is why integrity is essential if you are going to be a Broker because over time, people will trust you; some will trust you blindly, and you must make sure you don't betray their trust. Make sure that people wire money into your corporate account if it's not your money. Then, buy their property and be content with the commission you are being paid because a good name is better than silver or gold. Over time, even the money you're looking for, a good name will bring it to you. Often, we sell more than 10 million worth of land in Dubai in less than one year because of integrity. How many people do that in less than a year? Some trusted us with 550 acres of land, and gradually, we sold and paid their money, and the rest is history.

2. Buy Water Land; it appreciates better than Dry Land

Please write this down somewhere; water land appreciates better than dry land. Fortunately for me, the first land I was given to sell was water land, the 50 acres of land the man who needed my sales coaching entrusted to me.

The problem was that the land was waterlogged. Some of my friends, including those in the real estate business, told me it wouldn't work.

There is this quote at the back of my mind that encouraged me those days, "God will always give you the ability to do the impossible with what is available; any time you see what is available, goes for it". I just told them we would do the impossible with the 50 acres of waterlogged land that is available, and that was the beginning of our breakthrough story in the real estate business. Let me tell you why many of us don't make progress; it's because we look down on what God has already placed in our hands. Henceforth, I want you to start cultivating the habit of using what is available to do the impossible. At some point, we didn't have enough money, but we didn't give up, and that's why Gtext Homes became a multi-billion naira company today. When I hear people say we're a big company; you people are doing well, they don't know we had to start with what was available.

I did a thorough research about waterlogged land, and discovered that every big city in the world is near water. Kindly note that the big cities in the world are either near water, surrounded by water, divided by water or in front of the water. For instance, London is surrounded by water and divided by water. That's why we have the London Bridge. Also, places like Victoria Island in Nigeria. We started buying lands that faced the Lagoon and the Atlantic Ocean. That's why Lagos State lands have appreciated more than elsewhere in Africa. Lagos is the number one real estate in terms of return on investment in Africa, and Banana Island is the most expensive land in the world. New York is more significant, but they don't have land anymore. That's why floors are sold in Manhattan. Banana Island's 600 square metre of land goes for between two million to five million dollars.

Purchasing water land is mostly the best option, but please get advice from a mentor; you need someone to guide you, don't do this thing on your own. Do not do real estate without guidance from a successful mentor; you need someone to hold you by the hand.

3. Buy a bush that has a plan

Yes, you heard it, right? First, you must buy a bush that has a plan.

When buying land in the bush, what you must consider is the location. For example, instead of buying water land in Victoria Island, try the expensive Banana Island; you may not be able to afford it initially.

I started buying bushes in Ikorodu, Ibeju-Lekki, and Abuja. My secret was that I ensured I bought a marshy land close to the airport, hotel etc. I'm not just saying buy any bush; buy a bush with a plan. In the chapters above, I have discussed how to identify a land and location for land banking. Even when I started making it big from real estate, I bought more bush because I didn't have enough capital. Also, the city of today was yesterday's bush. Don't forget that there was a time in the 60s when Ikoyi, Lagos, was purely bush. Another similar example is where Transcorp Hilton Hotel, Abuja, is today.

You must understand that in real estate, you must pay it forward. That's how these things work. It is always the bush of today that turns into the city of tomorrow, so buy the bush now, and it will appreciate with time. Unfortunately, everybody wants to buy the city, and often, you can't even afford it.

As of 1985, one will call the government ridiculous and think, why will anyone venture into this kind of investment in bushy lands with little hope of development and exposure reaching the place soon? But today, Transcorp Hilton, Abuja, is standing on that land.

A good land banker is a man or woman turning a bush into a city. However, ensure you get a mentor to guide you because you don't want to buy one that has no plan.

This was why I bought some plots of land in Ibeju-Lekki a few years ago. I knew a new airport was coming there, a seaport and many other beautiful things. There are some of the properties I bought in Ibeju-Lekki for 1.5 million naira and 1 million naira six years ago, and now, they are going for 25 million and 30 million naira, respectively. See the margin.

Today, I'm not just a rich man, but I'm blessed. I always tell people I'm more sure of my tomorrow than today because of the investment I made years ago. Right, I am too sure of my tomorrow because that same property I told you I sold for 25 million naira today, I will still sell some of them for 200 million naira in the next 15 years. Land banking is how to secure your future. That is how you make the next generation's life better than yours. Make sure that you create a better generation, a better future than the one your parents gave you so that your children can say God bless my father, he's a great man, or God bless our mother, she's a great woman.

4. Pay in Instalment

Let me share my biological mother's story with you. She was a civil servant before she died.

She didn't have money but had to raise five children. I'm the 3rd child out of 5 children. I remember when I used to stay at my friend's place. After she died, they sent me out because they felt I was a burden to them. When I left their house, I became homeless in Lagos; the only place I could go was the house my mother bought in Sangotedo. Can you guess how much she bought that land?

That was the only land she left for her five children, the only place we could stay when she died.

She bought the land for eight thousand naira, and could not afford to pay for it all at once. She was asked to pay two thousand naira in each instalment. My adopted mother was also a friend who also lives in Lagos. She said, "Stephen, I used my five thousand naira salary to buy land. She continued like you guys but we managed to build our own houses. I'm thrilled that in your generation, people would rather purchase cars than land. They're myopic about their children and future generations".

A car is not an asset except if you use it for Uber. Please write this down; the best time to buy land is not today. It was yesterday. Another mistake people make is they wait for a particular location to develop before they buy. If you keep waiting, you're wasting your time. I will never forget this quote by Bill Gates that says "Smart people do not wait for the future; they create the future". What about you take it a step further by writing this vow with your name boldly written?

I, (Insert your name), make a vow today to create the future I want, and I'm not going to wait for the future to come and meet me.

I despise poverty. I hate seeing people as poor. I am not too fond of it when people are not doing everything in their power to become wealthy because I have seen poverty, I lost the most caring person in my life, my mum, to ovarian cancer, and I was in a position where I couldn't help her. Poverty is horrible, but if you are going to end poverty, you have to take action. You must be the person that creates the world they want. If God changed my story from poverty to wealth, I believe He can do more for you. Land banking changed my life. If you follow the secrets I'm sharing in this book, you will experience your breakthrough soon. Don't give up. You can start by paying in instalments. At Gtext Homes, we accept instalment payments too. If you deposit 500 000 naira every month, I will hold you by hand to guide you through this real estate journey.

I have somebody here in Dubai who gave me a gift of appreciation a few months ago. He said he could never have believed he could own a property because of the kind of money he was making. So he started with instalment payments. He said that when he paid for the land, which was seven million naira, he sold it for 25 million naira.

You can imagine how much the land has appreciated. You can start this journey today; it's up to you to make that decision right now. You have to be hungry for success to succeed.

I realised that once you start making land investment, money will come supernaturally. I don't know if you have noticed that. It's the same thing with building a house; when you start building, you will notice how money will supernaturally locate you to complete that house. It's divine; it's not explainable. So if you are ever going to own property, start with an instalment; start somewhere. With instalments, everyone can build something great. It was an instalment that our great-grandparents, mothers, and parents used to secure the future.

Will you take action today to secure the future for your generation too?

5. Get a property mentor

This is one of the most critical steps you need to take. Yes, you need a Property Mentor.

You have a Spiritual Mentor, right? I guess your answer is yes. Now, this is where many of us miss it. We have a Spiritual mentor, someone or a pastor that prays for us; nothing is wrong with that. I have a Spiritual Mentor too. But do you have a Property Mentor or an Investment Mentor? If yes, that's great. If not, you need to find one. It is also known as Prosperity Mentor, and the rule for mentorship is that the person must be successful. Have you noticed that poor people always get mentors that are poorer than them or at the same level as them? Some of you will say, I will never buy any property without my friend. Now the question is, is your friend poor or at the same financial level as you? Ensure you make a wise choice! Choose someone more successful than you; it's one of my secrets today. You cannot teach me if you don't have more results than me; that's my rule. I love mentorship, but my rule before I can have somebody to be my mentor is that what you're handling must be bigger than my own.

Some months ago, I was in a session with a new student of mine who is into real estate. He paid me twenty thousand dollars which he could afford because he is a prominent real estate company that has an extensive estate already, but he said, "Dr Stephen, I love the way you do real estate, I love the serenity, I love the structure you have around your business. You have it all over the world, yet everything is so structured. I want something like that too". How many of you have a mentor? The biggest problem with many of us is that we stumble into all these things without a mentor, nobody guiding us. It is no wonder why you've been losing money. This year alone, I have paid over 260,000 dollars to my mentors, so it's not only that I'm charging people to mentor them, but I also pay for mentorship. Grant Cardone is my Real Estate and Sales mentor; John Maxwell is my Leadership mentor, and Brain Tracy is my Sales mentor. Robert Kiyosaki is my Money mentor. I'm forever grateful to that man for helping me understand how to make and manage multiple income streams.

If you don't have people ahead of you, people who have done something bigger than you showing you the ropes, you will get overburdened by the pressure of what you're doing and get so stressed. What you're doing is no big deal; some people have done it bigger. To become wealthy, you must look for a mentor who can guide you through the whole journey. Ensure you get a property mentor as soon as possible. How do you get a mentor? It's either you pay, or you serve your mentor.

Some mentors do have coaching programs that pay for it, but if you don't have money to pay to serve them. Go and sell their property. That is how I started with my first property mentor in Nigeria. I was selling his property for him, and he was giving me a commission, and because I was loyal to him, he kept helping and showing me the ropes. Gtext Homes has a marketing program at www.gtextandassociates.com, go ahead and register and start promoting Gtext Home property. Wherever you are, whether in Nigeria, the U.S., London, Dubai, or Canada, we have properties in most of these locations you can sell. You may be among the top salespeople that will win an all-expense paid trip to any country we are going to that month.

During that trip, one of the things we do is sit down with everybody and start mentoring them because your success is my success. I have a few people who chatted me up on social media saying that they were deceived; they bought a property from a real estate company and are having challenges, asking if I can help to mentor them on how to overcome them. I'm surprised when they ask me such a question because they know Gtext Homes, left it and went elsewhere, only to come back when they start facing challenges. I don't know exactly what they expected me to do, maybe to fight that company. When it comes to mentorship, you will never find a perfect mentor, but focus on what you have come to learn.

6. Build a structure around your investment

Building a structure around your investment is essential to your journey to building a multi-billion naira real estate empire.

If you're going to become a property investor like me, ensure there's a structure around it. When you buy land, how do you structure it?

- Receipt of payment
- Deed of Assignment
- Survey plan

Our lawyers must prepare your Deed of Assignment and Survey in your name, but you have to pay separately.

7. Buy a serviced plot

Ensure you buy a serviced plot whether you're the one developing it or not. *A serviced plot is a plot of land in which the developer provides the internal road with a fence around the property and will provide infrastructure for that estate and good planning for the estate.* One of the biggest mistakes many people make is to buy a property that is not a serviced plot because it is cheap, and so before you know it, they never made provision for a road. Do you know that when we buy land now, 20 per cent of the land goes to the internal road layout, because we have to make sure we do a structured layout and town planning?

We plan each estate: where the road, hospital, kids' playground, mall etc., will be. When you buy land that is not a serviced plot, you're losing because the property will not appreciate.

Always buy land from a real estate company. If you buy land from a real estate company, you can take them to court when things don't go well. The Government or Court will force them to pay you back your money. But when you buy land from an individual, the first thing is holding on to that person. The person that stole the money from you has the right to tell the Judge that it will take him 50 years to pay you back. When you spend so much money to process a case, at the end of the day, there's no guarantee you will get anything back because the person can say to the Judge, "My Lord, I don't have the money, go and check I don't have anything. It will take me 50 years to pay this person back". What would you do?

THE FOUR FORMULAS YOU NEED TO SUCCEED IN LAND BANKING

1. Take more land banking risk despite previous losses

Yes, you must take the first step by practising the secrets I shared above. Let me tell you one secret, I have lost 120 million naira in real estate, but didn't share it with anyone until I recovered the money I lost in multiple folds.

In the Real Estate business just like every other business, it's all about taking risks. You won't always win, but if you have the right mentors. You will rarely have a loss. The more willing you're to take the risk, the more money you will make. That's how it works.

2. Add value to the land

I have mentioned this before. The reason why a land appreciates aside from the location it's because you added value to it. You can add value to land by building a fence around it and ensuring you buy land in a location with infrastructure plans like airports, hospitals, hotels etc.

3. Start from the level you are

This cannot be overemphasised. Start from where you are currently. Start today if you have 1 million naira to start your multi-billion real estate. Don't wait until you have 100 million naira to start.

4. Switch to rental income

At some point, you need to move to the next level, a rental property. Yes, rental property is very lucrative. Build or buy a house and rent it to tenants. Trust me, it's a significant investment.

In conclusion, starting land banking today is one of the best decisions you can ever make. If you follow these formulas and every other secret in this book, you will soon become a multi-billion land banker.

See you at the top!

CHAPTER 13
HOW I STARTED MY MULTI-BILLION NAIRA LAND BANKING EMPIRE WITHOUT CASH II

I realised that as you grow in your expertise and the more people know you or you gain more fans, most of them won't know your story. They don't know how you started; I mean, they begin to assume things. Ultimately, I didn't get here by luck.

In this chapter, I will share with you a couple of things I did to get to where I am today in the real estate sector.

One significant advantage of buying land close to a major city is that once there's a population explosion, the land you bought on the outskirts will start appreciating. The same thing is happening in Dubai; if you look at downtown Dubai, it's already congested, so you ask yourself, further down from downtown, where else can you buy land?

When doing land banking, you're not buying land so that you live there; you're buying land so that when the property appreciates, you will make a 100% return on investment. I have seen people who bought lands in millions and made billions a few years later and those who bought lands in thousands and made millions. **Kindly refer to the land banking stories I shared in Chapters 5 and 11.**

Five strategies you can use to create wealth in land banking

1. Buy land from significant cities

If you're buying land from your village, that's not land banking. Always buy land close to the city centre where property appreciates and where population growth is crazy. For instance, the housing deficit in Lagos is over five to seventy million. I always tell people I don't have a plot of land in my village, even as I write this book. I will do that someday. Yes, wise people will first build wealth where they can quickly get their return on investment. If I build a palace in my village, that one is to empower my people when I have made money. Have you noticed Obi Cubana's Oba in his home town is not as luxurious as his club in Abuja and Lagos?

Every time I look deeper when studying wealthy people, I always see what others are not seeing. I realised that before he buried his mother, he opened several hotel businesses, and all those his friends who came lodged in and paid for the hotel services. He made money from the hotels, and many people gave him money because they wanted to identify with him.

So when you hear about a rich man, look deeper to understand his story. Pastor Paul Adefarasin is also another example of doing land banking in a major city.

2. Buy bush land

I am surprised when I see young people buy cars when they don't have any landed property in their name. They always say, "Dr Stephen, but you own a car?" They always forget I bought my first car when I invested in landed properties. The car you see I use is an asset, not a liability. I have new businesses where those cars are used for marketing and logistic tools. When I started land banking, I started buying bushes, but I made millions and billions from those lands. Before I bought my first car, those days, most of my friends were mocking me because I didn't have a car, but I didn't mind. I was busy investing heavily in real estate, and today, it paid off. Today, I can buy as many cars as I want. Hitherto, I'm still investing more money in real estate. But, I'm being proactive about it.

Make sure you're spending your money wisely. The good thing about bush land is that it's more affordable than not bushy land. So, as you're starting in the real estate business, you should go for the bushy lands.

3. Take more risks in land banking

Regardless of your previous losses, if you want to make it big in land banking, you need to take more risks. However, get an experienced mentor for yourself, but I want you to take more risks this time. I've made billions from the real estate business, but I also want to let you know that I have lost up to 120 million naira in land banking. Yes, there's a probability of losing money in land banking, but when you find an experienced mentor, you won't lose much. I wouldn't have been here today if I decided to give up when I lost 120 million in land banking.

You see, those of us that they call wealthy, the riches or wealth that you see is a reward for our risk. Yes, **money is a reward for the risk taken by anybody.**

If you don't take risks, you can never be wealthy. I didn't say it on social media, and I'll tell you why I didn't. If I said it, many of you would have discouraged me, and I see this happening in Africa. I notice that the pity party behaviour of Africans only makes us poorer. If you lose, many of them will give you advice and discourage you, and if you don't take risks, you will remain poor. So one of my secrets is that I never announce my losses publicly until I've recovered the money more than ten times.

My wife and children call me blessed. My wife teaches my children to love their dad because she knows their dad has left an inheritance for them. She always says, "You may not know now what Stephen Akintayo has done for you all. Go and greet your daddy". That's how my wife trained our children always to say, "Daddy, I love you" and "You're the best daddy in the world" and some of you whose wife is not doing this may be because you have no inheritance for your children. So wake up and start building an inheritance for your children. The Bible says, Sarah calls Abraham Lord because he left an inheritance for the children they have not even given birth to.

4. Replicate wealth for your generation through land

banking

This is how you replicate wealth from one generation to the other. The principle of land banking, when applied, is how you transfer wealth from one generation to the other because, guess what? All these land banking strategies I'm sharing with you made me a multi-billionaire. What do you think my children will do when they grow up?

Of course, they will learn and practise the same principle of land banking I shared with you guys, and that's how generational wealth is built. You remember the story of Pastor Paul Adefarasin's father, how he bought land and rented it and how Pastor Paul learnt the same principle and bought an acre of land. So land banking is one of the easiest ways to replicate wealth for your generation.

5. Switch to rental income

How do you switch to rental income? After keeping your land for about 5-10 years, it's advisable to sell a portion of the land and build on the rest to rent it out and make more money. That way, you've created cash flow, which is also why I always tell people not to buy up to two plots of land. Most times is not the best option; sometimes, it's not the best option for you.

It would be best if you bought more plots of land; maybe you could spread the payment between three to six months. So that at the end of the day, you may decide to sell two plots of land and build on the remaining two. When you're done building and renting it out to tenants. You can start making huge money from the rented properties. We have started building our green and smart estate at Gtext Homes. The builders are working day and night. We're going to be doing over a thousand units. It will be launched in less than two years. But don't forget you have to start from where you're. Some of my mates who are waiting to buy lands at perfect locations are still waiting to date.

CHAPTER 14
Dear Potential Billionaire, Humbly Start With Mini Estate: The How

It is astounding how many individuals say they cannot return to Nigeria if they have the opportunity to leave. I hear many say there is nothing in Nigeria, and they cannot make it here. Yes, Nigeria has its challenges, but you can only become what you allow your mind to believe. The mind is a critical factor in determining how successful we will be and where. If you think you can't become wealthy in Nigeria, you're right, but if you are like me, that vowed when I was a student and said if there is a legal way people make it in this country, then I would explore that option and I will also make it here and to the glory of God I did. We started our business fourteen years ago with one thousand naira, and today we are a multi-billion corporation that has expanded to four major continents of the world, Nigeria, Dubai, the United States and the United Kingdom. So, your mind has much to do with becoming whom you desire to be.

In this chapter, I will discuss how to become a billionaire by owning a mini estate through land banking.

Again, land banking is the process of aggregating land for future sales or development. That means I buy a piece of land and leave it for some years, and the goal is to build houses or resell them when the price eventually increases.

I purchased a land property six years ago in Ikorodu for land banking. Although the environment is already developed, people live around the area, but I knew I would need to pump much money into the land because it is a wet area to sand fill and make it viable as an estate. When we bought the land at that time, we sold it for seven hundred and fifty thousand naira, and eight years later, the same land is now sold for eight to ten million naira. Can you see the difference? That's land banking. The next thing we are doing is building a hundred housing units on the land. So what have I done?

First, I have made money from land banking because I bought the land, left it for eight years, and the value increased. Not only did the value increase for not doing anything, but I also added value to it. I also did the road that led to the place because when I bought it, we couldn't get to the site; it was bushy and waterlogged. I spent hundreds of millions to sand fill it and to do the fencing. So I have added value to the estate. How can you also do the same? How can you buy land and leave it for five to ten years? The value would have been appreciated, and even if you do not have money for development, just as we have done, we left it for years, and now the money we realised from the land we are using to build the estate, you can do the same also.

That is wisdom; if you are doing land banking, only sell some of your lands even if you need money. Many people do this; because they are trying to run an estate structure as a business, so as soon as they hear that the value has increased, they go ahead to sell all the land, and at the end of the day, they have nothing to show forth. May you not use your hand to point to where you sold, and may you not be a tenant in a land you used to own. So, you have to be smart when you want to do land banking. I hope you are getting some value.

Someone said if you want to hide something from a black man, put it in a book he will not read it; put it in a seminar, he will not attend, but put it into entertainment, and he will jump at it. We need to change that. We need to start changing the narrative that Africans are intelligent and innovative and value knowledge. That's what will help us learn how to get wealth.

FIVE MAJOR WAYS TO START MINI ESTATE

1. Have an investment budget.

One of the ways to achieve this is to be determined and start saving. The biggest challenge I have seen with us as Africans is that we think wealth creation is sudden, luck, or it happens overnight. Some of the most annoying conversations I have had with people I shared my contact with ask me questions like how do I become a billionaire like you, as if it is magic. There is no such thing. Any attempt to become rich suddenly only lengthens your journey to success. There is no shortcut to success. You can reduce the timeline by having a mentor, but there is no shortcut.

It would help if you were disciplined enough not to eat with five fingers. When I bought this same land in Ikorodu, I was still driving a Toyota Rav4, the first car I had in my life. When I go to meetings, people look at me and mock me, saying, "You are a developer and are still driving this kind of car." I knew where I was going, so I had to be disciplined and proactive.

"Rich people do what their mates are not doing today, so they can afford what their mates cannot afford tomorrow."

Many people want to become rich, but they are not ready to follow the principles of wealth. It would help if you were disciplined. These are some of the secrets of wealthy people. Even when they live a luxurious life, it is for business. You have to be disciplined to start paying yourself. So, in every money you make, you must cultivate the habit of saving out of it, no matter how little it is.

Note that money is never enough, so you have to learn how to save from it. For example, you must learn to cut your coat according to your material, not your size, so you can pay yourself first by saving.

There are two types of people in the world, the Tenant and the Landlord. **"Landlords make money in their sleep because the tenants go to work for them."** So take land banking seriously first by saving to have an investment budget.

When you see a wealthy man, you see an opportunity that meets preparation. The person was prepared for the investment before it came. Sometimes, people get the opportunity to become landowners but cannot because they are not disciplined to save. They always claim that money is not enough; the truth is, it will never be enough.

2. **Look for a significant development (estate) with a plan and invest in it.**

When I got to Ikorodu that year, I saw an extensive development with over two fifty acres, and the owner said to me, I can give you fifty acres; as you sell, you pay. And that's how I started.

If you are proud, you can never become rich. Many of the opportunities that will make you wealthy will come as problems. Many opportunities that will give you money will not look like it; it will not make sense. I sought people's counsel about that property, and they said I should not try it because I could not afford it, mainly because it was waterlogged.

So, look for something big and invest in it. For example, you can purchase five acres of land today and leave it there for the next five years, after which you can sell 2.5 acres. The profit you will make is enough to start building houses on the remaining acres of land, and you will still sell the house. That is how rich people think. Also, this is how wealth and prosperity are birth.

Starting your estate will cost a considerable amount of money, so you can lean on those who have gone ahead of you. I also bought from someone ahead to reduce my stress because the acquisition problem is off it. So at the beginning of starting your estate, you are yet to build the capacity for property acquisition, and if care is not taken, you will be swindled by land grabbers (Omo Onile). However, you do not have to go through that stress, so it will be better to look for a bigger estate with a well-structured plan, buy from it, and start your journey there.

3. Buy from an estate that is well structured.

Buy about one to five acres, do not buy less than one acre if the plan is for a mini estate. If you want to buy for yourself, you can go for fewer plots of land. Buy in bulk for the estate.

4. Pay in instalments.

Deposit the amount you can afford, and pay the rest gradually. This is one of the most potent ways of owning property. Many of the estates we own today were bought and paid in instalments. For some, it took us months and some years to complete the payment. I was not this rich when I started the business; I told you I started with one thousand naira. We did not start with money. We started with paying in instalments.

Take this warning, only buy what is realistically possible for you to afford, and do not be greedy. If you know you cannot afford millions, buy what you can and will not choke you. Know what you can afford and pursue it.

5. Buy the land even if it has no Certificate of Occupancy (C of O) title.

Most of the time, the lands that have C of O are more expensive, and you may not be able to afford it, but if you can afford it, please buy lands that have C of O only. The estate in Ikorodu did not have a C of O when I bought it, so I also started that way. If you get land that does not have a C of O, you can then do the Registered Survey, after which you can apply for your C of O. It will be cheaper that way.

Also, do not buy a property under acquisition; if it is under acquisition, make sure that the acquisition is not a committed one or the acquisition is for residential houses. This is how you can start your mini estate. There is a saying that slow and steady wins the race. Usually, if you build an estate on land under residential acquisition, the government will ask you to rectify, and you will still end up owning your land.

I hope you have gotten value. See you in the next chapter.

PART FIVE
WEALTH TRANSITION IN REAL ESTATE

CHAPTER 15
Moving From Millions To Billions Using Land Banking I: My Transition Story Into 8-Figures

While growing up, I used to come from school to Victoria Island (VI), Lagos, Nigeria. I remember the whole place was by a beach, a very flooded area currently called Eko Atlantic, a very affluent place filled with beautiful skyscrapers of 20-50 story buildings, but it wasn't always this way. People used to disdain VI back then due to so much flooding around its surroundings. However, those who didn't invest in VI are regrettably sorry; why is it that, they were too short-sighted to see the immense opportunity and great potential for wealth creation hidden within and beneath its environs. Now, VI is such a gold mine worth millions and billions of dollars.

The principles that guarantee your successful transition into land banking are as follows;

1. Locate the right mentor: Who is the right mentor? The right mentor has proven success in a dream, vision or plan you hope to accomplish in the future. Never follow just anyone; follow only those who have proven success in the area in which you desire results. You can't do it on your own; you need mentors, people who know the market, who know how the environment works, and who will give you guidance and counsel.

2. Look for the outskirts of a major city to invest in: The reason for this is because every densely populated city grows towards the outskirts, and a lot of people will not be able to afford land or houses in the city and will look for affordable ones in its surroundings. Once you can buy those properties around those fringes or places that are not yet developed in that part of the city, your wealth creation journey starts once development begins to creep in.

3. Buy land when it's low in value and cost less and leave the land for a long time to appreciate, then sell it at a great price afterwards: Many people buy land for the euphoria of wanting to build a house of their own, this is good in itself, but will not ultimately guarantee your wealth in land banking. One of the core and most profitable reasons to buy land is for investment so that the land can appreciate and you can sell it for a much higher price. I met a man who was 87 years of age, and at the time we met, he told me how he was given 6 plots of land in Surulere 40-something years ago, but he turned down the offer because the place was too bushy. He wanted a place more developed; sadly, that decision was one of the biggest regrets of his life. Abraham Lincoln said, "One of the best ways to predict the future is to create it". If you keep looking at issues from the perspective of "I want a house today. I want it already developed", the first challenge you'll encounter is that you may not be able to afford that property. Properties are much more expensive now, especially in Lagos. Many people have fallen victim to get-rich-quick schemes and have been swindled. The key is to exercise a little patience in your investments and watch them bring unprecedented wealth and prestige.

Examples of those who invested in land banking and succeeded:

1. Pastor Paul Adefarasin

We've shared much about his story in the previous chapters and will not dwell so much on it.

2. The CEO and Chairman of Air Peace, Allen Onyema

He shared how land banking was the secret of his wealth. He was able to start his Airline from some of the money he made selling land at Abule Egba as well as some land at Ibeju-Lekki, both in Lagos State. As a lawyer, people started giving him land to sell, and as he was selling, he was making money. One of the secrets and principles Allen Onyema applies is still the same; because Ikeja was so expensive several years ago, and so many people couldn't afford properties or lands there, people resorted to buying land from him at Abule Egba. Most of the income he generated resulted from buying land from families and reselling it when the land had increased in value. Not every wealthy and successful person got their money illegally; some are very legitimate.

Sometimes, you'll need to look inwards and say, "What model am I using? How am I living my life? What strategy do I have to build great wealth so that the future will not be full of regrets?" Money will never be enough, so it's actually out of not having enough that you will have to struggle to find a way to still invest in land banking. You cannot build wealth without investing in land banking. Buy it at the level you can buy it.

3. The General Overseer of RCCG, Pastor E. A. Adeboye

When he bought the land, it was only six thousand naira, not a very nice site, but it was what they could afford at the time. However, buying property in that exact location costs millions of naira today. So when it comes to land banking, you won't succeed if you keep basing your decisions on what you see, but it may be the risk you need to take for an enviable destiny.

4. Dr Stephen Akintayo, GMD/CEO of Gtext Holdings

In 2012, when I started selling Shimawa, Lagos State, for another company I used to be a marketer and a broker for, the land was going for 550,000 naira. But today, those places cost millions of naira because somebody had the foresight. I helped some of those who invested through me. They invested 1.5 million naira, and today, the property is worth nine million.

Like I said earlier, you will never have enough money to start real estate. Start with what you have and where you are. The beautiful thing about land banking is that you can pay gradually, either three or six months instalments, and then wait until things get favourable.

CHAPTER 16
Moving From Millions To Billions Using Land Banking II

To begin with, for you to harness the wealth in this chapter, you must have started land banking. One of the significant ways to acquire wealth is through Land Banking. If you have started. How do you now move forward or scale your land banking business?

The first step is to start with people who have done something similar and ask them to teach you so you can replicate something similar.

5 Secrets on Moving from Millions to Billions in Land Banking

1. **Location**

Ensure you buy your land in a place that appreciates. When doing land banking, one of the strategies we consider is a location where there's a population explosion and, housing deficiency.

According to Business Day, over 600 people move to Lagos, and less than 50 per cent of them go back. Hence, because of the population explosion in Lagos, you will always get a return on investment. It doesn't matter where you get to land in Lagos; you will get a return on investment. That puts you in an excellent position to get land banking in Lagos.

The top hot locations in Nigeria are:
- Lagos State
- Abuja
- Port Harcourt
- Ogun State: Any part of Ogun state that has a boundary with Lagos.

- Oyo State: Lagos-Ibadan expressway is hot cake too.

How to know the right location (Location Indicators):
- It should not be too far or close to the expressway or tiled road.
- It should be close to industrial factories.
- It should be close to major religious gatherings.

2. Make full payment

Make sure you pay in full for the properties you're buying. Until you're done paying and get a document called 'Deed of Assignment', you do not yet own the land. Let me share with you this quote by Franklin Delano Roosevelt.

"Real estate cannot be lost or stolen, nor can it be carried away. Purchased with common sense, paid for in full, and managed with reasonable care, it is about the safest investment in the world."

Paying in full is a powerful way to secure your land/properties. Endeavour to do it as fast as possible because if any issue comes up, the person that sold the land to you will win because you have not yet completed your payment or, in some cases, the value of the land has appreciated, and you have to pay maybe 10 times more than your initial payment.

Someone I know was slow in completing his land payment, and by the time he was done paying, the land had appreciated from 8 million naira to 20 million naira. Unfortunately, they refunded him his money. These are potent secrets nobody can tell you; I'm talking from experience. I have lost 120 million in real estate, but I have also made billions from real estate.

3. Take possession and perfect the title of your property

Two ways to take possession of your property:
- Document Possession: Get your Deed of Assignment and Survey for that land.
- Develop the land: Start building something on the land. It could be a fence. Just find a way to take some form of possession.

Also, perfect your titles. I'm not kidding you. Some of those in the diaspora always forget this when investing in land banking. They always forget to request it because they don't live in the country they bought the land from. However, I'm glad that most of them are now taking advantage of land banking recently, unlike before.

4. Buy the landed property or house in bulk

There is no bigger secret than you buying landed properties in bulk. If you buy only one plot, you might regret it later. But if you buy two or three plots, ten years down the line, you could sell one plot and use the money from one plot to develop the other plots. That is one of the biggest mistakes people have made in land banking. They got a good location, and everything was perfect, but they didn't buy enough land because they were afraid or, in some cases, didn't have enough money. If you don't have the money, at least you know in your heart that that was all you could afford at that time, and it won't be that painful, unlike when you had the money and didn't buy the land.

5. Raise capital by reselling to other people

That is one of the most potent principles you need to know about success in real estate. That is how success works, and you want to replicate this model. I'll give you an example: Am I making money from real estate? Yes, but guess what? I'm making more money from people trying to learn real estate from me. For instance, if you want to start your estate like we do at Gtext Homes, or you want to start your own real estate development company, I will charge you 20,000 USD.

I have made money doing real estate, but I'm making a lot more money by teaching the lessons I learned. Now you can start by telling your friends to try out real estate as they earn commission between the range of five to ten percent from Gtext Homes. We have people earning 2 - 10 million naira every month from commission.

You know what? They are also making money through land banking, but aside from land banking, they also make more money from referring people. So from that, they can raise capital to expand their land banking empire. Imagine, for instance, that you bought one acre of land in Ibeju-Lekki, but your dream is to own a hundred acres of land on Victoria Island. From the 5 acres or 10 acres of land you bought, meet your friends, and show them your receipt or Deed of Assignment, so they will know you were not scammed. Most of them will also ask you to show them the place they want to buy. You don't need to tell them you're earning a commission, but gradually you'll get a 10% commission. You can then use your 10% to buy more land and expand. If you do this for 10 years, I promise you cannot have less than 100 plots of land to your name, and I promise you that 100 plots of land cannot be less than three billion naira. Try it!

CHAPTER 17
Building Wealth Through Land Banking.

Land Banking is a high-risk investment that is worth it. No type of business or investment will give you the type of return on investment that land banking can give you.

As I mentioned earlier, you need a mentor to guide you when starting in the real estate business; otherwise, it may not be a successful venture for you, or you might meet fraudsters.

If the real estate company you're dealing with is not putting a face to the business,, you're in trouble. The real estate business is not a Tech business because the property you bought is tangible; it's something you can see. So make sure that you're dealing with a credible organisation.

Also, ensure that the owners are willing to put their face to what they are doing; otherwise, when issues occur, you can't even go out on social media and say you sent your money to a particular real estate company and that they have disappeared. Also, always verify the history of the real estate company before investing your money. How long has this company existed? What is the history of this organisation? How did they start their business? When you research them properly, you can find something tangible to hold on to.

If you google Gtext Homes, you will get every information you need about our business, including our history. We started 14 years ago as a Bulk SMS company before we ventured into real estate 7 years ago. It's also good to note that when searching for a credible real estate company to deal with, understand that you don't just rush into it, probably because you see everywhere that they are the best. No, it would help if you did your research because it's your money at the end of the day, and you want to invest in something that will bring much return on investment for you.

My student bought land in Nicon Estate, Lekki Phase 2 Lagos State, for 12 million naira. 15 years later, we sold the land for 220 million naira. That's where top shots like Alibaba reside. You can see how lucrative the real estate business can be. The land was all water 15 years ago; they paddled a canoe the day he went to see the land. No investment can yield such a return on investment except land banking.

The good thing is that he invested with the right company. Once you make your investment with the right company, you go to sleep. So if you do land banking with the right company, you don't need to put any more money into it once you make the initial investment, it's a sure deal years later.

Cryptocurrency has crashed many times, and many people didn't see it coming each time it happened. But you don't have that issue with land banking; you do it once, and it remains there.

Sometimes you hear that people are rich, but you don't even know the story; you don't know what they did, and many of us continue this circle. The truth is that you can fall off a ladder by accident, but can't climb one by accident. If you will be rich, there is a process, except you want to do it illegitimately. If you want to be legitimately wealthy, some processes are viable that are verified, which many people have used.

I am worried for our generation, which is one of the reasons I am writing this book and hosting all the webinars I often do. If our generation is not careful, we will become paupers in the end because we are not investing. We are just using money as we like. So it's time to start saving for land banking or, tell those who want to lavish money on you to 'freak' your account with money for real estate.

You have to be intentional about it. A car is a liability unless you're using it for Uber; the same thing to a house. If you're not renting it to tenants, then it's a liability. Did you know that if you buy a Rolls Royce today, drive it out of the dealer's shop, and return it that same day, the price would have depreciated by 25%? But when you buy land today, 5 - 10 years down the line, the value would have gone higher and higher when it comes to land. This is why we need to begin to encourage our generation to start investing.

I started my own business with 1000 naira. 14 years later, we have built a multi-billion empire. We have offices now in Dubai, the U.K, and the U.S. We also have different offices in Nigeria. The office addresses will be stated at the end of this book.

But before we got to this level, I can recall some years back, one of my friends used to laugh at me because I usually entered public transport. But then, I was busy investing in my real estate business, and the story has changed. I'm not saying you should not buy a car or house if you need it; I am only saying you should learn to save and invest your money. Don't compare yourself with wealthy people. Some rich people who have Rolls Royce rent it out to people doing their weddings or other significant occasions.

The question is, how is that car generating more money for you? If you watch rich people closely, **they only spend the third generation of their investment.** So let me explain what I mean by the third generation of your investment.

Let's say you made 10 million naira from a deal. Instead of 'freaking' people's accounts with that money, you decided to buy land. Now you bought land for 10 million naira and left it for 5 years. Guess what? The value has probably appreciated to 100 million naira. Let's say you sell half the plot for 50 million naira; that's the *first generation wealth.* If you use the 50 million naira to build 5 units of a 2-bedroom apartment, the money you will make from the rent becomes the *second generation wealth.* From the rental income you made, if you buy another land and build another house and rent it out again, the proceeds are called *third generation wealth.* Then from your third generation wealth, you can start 'freaking' people's accounts.

"Smart investors only spend the third generation of their money, not the first."

So I know you may be asking yourself right now, what if I am earning between fifty thousand to hundred thousand naira monthly? How am I supposed to start land banking since it's expensive? So first, you need to understand your financial level right now. So if your income is between fifty thousand to a hundred thousand naira monthly, your priority is to do these types of investment:

The first one is to SAVE, and the second one is to make a MENTAL INVESTMENT. Mental investment means investing part of the money you saved in buying a course or learning various sources of investment so that when the money becomes bulk you don't end up being duped because you went into the wrong investment.

There are three types of investment you can make:

- **Low-Risk Investment:**

This type of investment gives you between 2 - 7% annual returns.

- **Mid-Risk Investment:**

This type of investment gives you between 10 - 15% annual returns.

- **High-Risk Investment:**

This type of investment gives you above 20% annual returns.

So, when your income is low, you need to start learning these different types of investments to know which one to invest in when the money becomes much. You can also invest in learning how to market real estate, start trading, or do cryptocurrency yourself.

At Gtext Homes, we made over 200 billion naira in commission in 2021. We have brokers from all over the world selling lands and properties for us and making big commissions for themselves, including unemployed graduates, and we're proud of that.

If you'd like to be part of the team that sells lands or houses and get commission, called Gtext and Associates, visit www.gtextandassociates.com to register. Most of our brokers started from nothing; now, most are millionaires. Some have enjoyed an all-expense paid trip to Dubai and Maldives sponsored by Gtext Homes.

"The secret is starting from where you are."

You may have a rich network of people who can buy the properties from you. Your network is your net worth. All you need to do is package yourself well, learn how to sell real estate to someone or maybe do digital marketing training on how to sell with Facebook and Instagram Ads, and before you know what is happening, people will start visiting your social media page to buy landed properties from you. Henceforth start using social media as a great tool to promote your business.

I always tell people this: I wasn't born rich. My mother was a civil servant, and my father's business had crumbled before I was even born in the Northern part of Nigeria. But I stood my ground and started looking for ways to become wealthy. I once sent a Cover Letter to several companies stating, "Do not pay me until I'm able to add value to your company". So yes I didn't get a job, but from there, I continued with my bulk SMS business and later started selling lands for real estate companies, earning commissions I used to start my own, and today the story has changed.

In 2021, we announced that we will provide 100,000 jobs for unemployed citizens through the Gtext and Associates program for free. At the moment, over 8,000 individuals have registered. They get a 10% commission for any property/land they sell to people, 5% directly to them and 2% - 3% for the all-expense paid trips. In January 2022, we also gave two of our highest-selling marketers brand-new cars. You can go to Gtext Homes or Gtext and Associates' social media platforms, and you will find the screenshots of those we have paid.

Anytime you buy properties from Gtext Homes, we ensure we send all your documents to you anywhere in the world, and don't send them to third parties; nobody is collecting them on your behalf to avoid stories touching the heart.

Some people have asked me this, "Dr. Stephen, what about in a situation where I am not interested in buying land or a house, I just want to drop a certain amount of money and expect a return on investment because I believe in what your company is doing". Yes, you can do that, because Gtext Homes has a program for people who only want to invest money, but note that the return on investment is yearly not monthly or quarterly. So it is not a Ponzi scheme; rather, we are doing a legitimate business and building a stable business.

Forex Trading or Cryptocurrency might give you a monthly return on investment, but it's not stable; it can crash at any time. Most of these businesses didn't start as Ponzi; they only made unrealistic promises they could not fulfil. So by all means, avoid any real estate company or business that promises you a massive return on investment.

For the ladies, I will advise that you use the money you want to use to buy bone-straight hair to invest in real estate first. Then, when the return on investment comes, you can go ahead and buy it. Make sure your destiny is straight first before you buy bone straight. Laughs!

I am so happy that God has used me to mentor many people in the real estate sector. There is a female mentee of mine with tremendous results as well. We met when she was 24 years old; she's now 29 years old. When she met me, she didn't have a job, so I advised her to go into the real estate business to sell lands and start making commissions. When we met at a seminar in 2021, she told me she has made so much money from the real estate business and has plots of land in her name. Wow, is this not interesting? At 29 years old? She also bought land for her mum.

Of course, the real estate business is not an overnight success. You have to be consistent and patient. The payday will come sooner than you expected.

In conclusion, no matter the level you're at, you can start a real estate business. If you have nothing, register for the Gtext and Associates program and you will be taught how to start earning big commissions from our properties and lands. If you have up to 5 million nairas, you can invest and get land to start building your land banking empire. There's something for everybody. We built our business structure in such a way that it could accommodate everybody.

Trust me, if I could build a multi-billion land banking business from scratch, you can do better if you practise all the secrets I have shared with you in this book.

CHAPTER 18
My Multi-Billion Evolving In Land Banking

I have built a multi-billion real estate empire because I decided to take a risk against what everybody said to me. Today, I ask myself why people fail to buy property because somebody told them not to buy it. Years later, they will start lamenting, saying, "You know I wanted to buy that property, but my friends and family said I shouldn't buy it". If I had listened to those people who loved me and gave me advice just out of care and love, I wouldn't be here today. Many of you have lost the opportunity to be millionaires and multi-millionaires because you took advice from people who do not have results. You took their advice because they loved and cared for you, but they don't have results in the area where you are trying to build wealth.

I remember one of my mentors when I started real estate. He was the first property I started promoting, and my family members told me not to because the land was waterlogged. On a specific day, I visited him to tell him about the issues I was facing; he looked at me, smiled and said, "Are you sure you are ready for Real Estate, this young man?" And he laughed. According to him, I didn't have what it takes to succeed in real estate, and this takes me to a quote that you should note down and never forget.

"Everybody has the right to doubt you, but you better not doubt yourself."

If you join the camp of people doubting you, your capacity, the possibility of you getting there, and whether you can do it or not, you will be in trouble. Let me tell you a secret I do. I always, often, listen to my critics and prove them wrong. It is essential to listen to them and hear what they say about you, so you can prove them wrong. Once you prove them wrong, people will respect you and give you the honour you deserve. That is because they doubted you and didn't believe you could pull it off, but you did.

A Real Estate broker shared with me sometime ago how he had a client trying to buy a property, and the client was complaining bitterly about how the one he bought from another company was waterlogged, and he felt so disappointed. He reached out to me, seeking what to tell the client. I laughed so hard, as you know, because the client had bought from another company, and he was trying to convince the person to buy our property, but the person was already bitterly complaining about the previous one he bought. I told him that a wet area or a property close to the water appreciates better. I said go and tell him that even though he didn't buy that property from us, if he's smart, he should keep that property because waterlogged properties appreciate faster than dry land.

I told you already that the biggest cities in the world are always close to water.

1. New York

Manhattan is an Island. Houses in Manhattan are the most expensive properties in the world. Suppose you're looking for the most expensive properties in the world. A studio apartment barely 6ft by 6ft in Manhattan costs more than 2 million dollars, and that is the most expensive. Years ago, when Jacobs Axton and John D. Rockefeller started the Manhattan Project, nobody wanted to participate in it because it was a marshy land. But, John D. Rockefeller saw the opportunity to build a mega global city in Manhattan. Today, Wall Street, where the highest amount of money in the world is made, is in Manhattan.

2. London

London is not only surrounded by water but is full of rivers and all types of water.

3. Paris

It is divided by water.

4. Dubai

In Dubai, people leave the desert and go to build artificial islands. An example is Burj Al Arab. Just look at the Dubai Skyline, and you will see that the place is closer to water. In Dubai, the most expensive areas are the islands.

That is the power of a waterlogged land. The day you want to buy such land, everybody around you will say you shouldn't do it. You wouldn't have the courage to say what I have told you in this book and tell them, "I believe in it, and I am going to try it out". Also, buy this book for your friends and family members, so they can have the same understanding as you and support you when you want to make these decisions.

If you are married, don't read alone; let your spouse join you so that you can make investment decisions together. If not, you both will go in opposite directions when it comes to investing in land banking. Adequate research will guide you both through when planning an investment. When the majority face a direction, you have to be careful, do your research and know the right thing to do.

"There is no poverty anywhere; there are only ignorant people who are only poor because they are ignorant."

FACTORS THAT MADE ME BUILD WEALTH IN LAND BANKING

1. Population growth

A factor that made me become a billionaire in land banking is that I sourced for population growth in the areas I was buying a piece of land. I looked at the sources of population increase and investment. I don't buy land in a place where nothing is driving the population increase. A source of population growth is job creation. For instance, in Ibeju-Lekki, we have the Dangote refinery, the Deep Seaport, the Free Trade Zone etc. All these are guaranteed avenues for job creation in that location, and people will migrate there because they are searching for jobs.

"Population growth is the ultimate driver of property prices."

An example is Dubai. Property prices skyrocketed in Dubai just because of Expo 2020. So with that, people were visiting Dubai, which increased property prices. Another factor is good roads.

One of the factors that drive population growth is the availability of land. For example, Ikorodu, Lagos, is one of the places I bought a land, because I realised that all the other aspects of Lagos were maxed out. There was no more land, and people were forced to move to Ikorodu. I researched and discovered that more people were moving to Ikorodu and owning properties. There is population growth now because other aspects of Lagos are getting maxed out, and are more expensive for people, so people are looking for other areas to move into and buy properties at a cheaper rate.

2. Security
This is also very crucial when investing in land banking. People want to move to places that are secure and peaceful.

3. Town planning
This is also important as well. We have planned all our estates across our 6 locations in Nigeria, and we noticed that anywhere Gtext Homes starts an estate, in a matter of six months, other people start an estate around us. The value of that location goes up because Gtext Homes is around that place. That happens because everybody understands that Gtext Homes is building Green and Smart Homes, and many would say, "My land is close to that company building Green and Smart Homes". Quite funny right?

That has made us negotiate always to buy enough land because we realised that if we go back to the family after we have launched the estate to buy more, they would say, "We didn't know you people are this big. We have heard you're a big company". Hence, they would increase the price to double what we bought before.

Even the companies we involve in the town planning, we ensure they do an excellent structure and layout because we realised that when we started interlocking our estates, other companies around the area started increasing their prices because they know a well-structured estate is coming around the neighbourhood.

4. **Avoid waste**

I had to cut down on waste. In the last four years, I've not bought a new car for myself. Many people don't know how hard I am on myself. I am so conservative, and one of the reasons is that I came from an impoverished background.

Some years ago, one of our leaders took company funds to organize my birthday party. They designed a big flyer for me and called a band to play. When I arrived at the branch, I had to ask them to investigate it, and he was fired immediately. You can not use company funds to do a flyer and call a band to come and sing for me. If you used your funds to do it, there's nothing I can do against it, but no company funds. That is a waste!

When I did my wedding, I did not do it big. I got married 10 years ago, and I did not do 'asoebi' (In Nigeria, it is a particular type of cloth that people sell when they are trying to do a burial, wedding or any special occasion. Everybody attending that occasion contributes money to buy those clothes, and at the event, everybody wears the same kind of cloth). I remember telling my wife that nobody was under pressure to buy any 'asoebi' from me because I was getting married. I changed that norm. I did not ask anybody to do that so when they were doing their wedding, they would not tell me I had to buy their own 'asoebi', because I didn't tell them to buy mine. You will also be glad to know that I did not do a big reception 10 years ago when I got married. We did it in my living room after we came back from the Court wedding, and we were less than 20 people. Guess what? Everybody had food to take home because we were less than 20, which was majorly my staff.

I did all that to reduce my cost. God hates waste. Many people cannot afford real estate that they are wasteful. They always shout, "Oh, it's too expensive; I cannot afford it". It's not true; it is because you are wasteful. In the same way, you are complaining that you cannot afford to buy two plots of land, but you have bought designers when your life is not yet designed. Many ladies are buying bone-straight hair when their destiny is not straight.

Likewise, if you have a car and don't have land in your name, you are being bewitched. Like people would say, "They are doing you from your village". Some people are spiritually attacking you if you have a car and you don't have a property or a plot of land in your name.

When you buy a car, even if it's a brand new car, and you drive it from the parking lot, it has lost 25 per cent of its value. In other words, if you buy a brand new BMW and decide to drive it out after paying for it and getting your receipt, and returning it 30 minutes later, it has lost 25 per cent of its value. Meanwhile, if you buy land in less than a year in some locations, it appreciates by 25 - 50 per cent. So, why are you wasteful?

I say this a lot, **"Africans are poor because we are wasteful"**. We always buy what we don't need to impress people that don't care. I am an African, and I know what I am saying. That is why we are poor because we're trying to impress people. We are trying to make people think we are friendly and good people; meanwhile, they don't care.

5. Overcome the need to please people

I did a training some years ago, and a man insisted on seeing me after the training. He came into my office, and when he had time off, he was almost kneeling saying, "Dr Stephen, I want to apologise to you; I'm sorry. I want you to forgive me". "What did you do?" I asked him. He replied, "Sir, this is not the first time

I am learning about you. I know you when you started your company almost 10 years ago, and there was a day I called you all manner of names. I called you devil, 419 etc. Forgive me because if I had known you would be this successful, if I had known that it was just a phase of your business and that you were still going to make it, I would not have spoken that way,". I said to him, "I forgive you because I can't even hold you accountable for something I don't even remember". I prayed for him and thanked him for coming back to say those words to me.

So, why do you need to please people who don't care? People cannot be pleased, so don't waste your time trying.

"The day you overcome the need to please human beings is the day you have overcome poverty by 50%."

I didn't become this successful financially until I did this. I reached a point in my life where I didn't care about what people thought of me. I believe it is their opinion, and they are entitled to it. You will not live and be free if you are too bothered about what people think and say about you. You need freedom. You need to know that human beings will just talk for talking sake.

One day, somebody posted on his Facebook timeline and said, "This Stephen, I don't like the man. I have never met him, but I just don't like him". You can imagine, someone hasn't met me before and he doesn't like me. That is human beings for you. Well, that is his opinion. I like myself a lot. I always say, "If you are taller than me, you're too tall. If you are darker than me, you're too dark. If you are fairer than me, you're too fair. If you are fatter than me, you are too fat. If you are slimmer than me, you are too slim. I am the perfect image of God. If you have never seen how God looks, check me out, and see how He looks". I love myself. If you don't like me to do business with me, you have the right not to, and I will not hold you against it.

6. Apply knowledge

Do you know knowledge does not make you rich? In fact, in

some cases it makes you poor. If knowledge makes you rich, Professors will be the wealthiest human beings in this world. But, you know, there is a massive difference between Professors and Entrepreneurs. That's why sometimes a person who never went to a university is the owner of a university. In other words, he has never been to a university but now owns one and pays Professors. That is because Professors study for studying sake and never take action, while Entrepreneurs take action. That's the difference, and it's the same between the rich and the poor. The poor keep hearing and learning but never take any steps.

Most of them say they have been following me for 2 - 5 years but haven't bought any land yet. When they meet me, they will begin ranting about how they have been following me for seven years as if it's an achievement. What have you done in those several years? That's the achievement. What action did you take from what I have taught? To you reading this book, what action will you take from the knowledge contained in this book?

7. Raise your budget

You have to raise your budget to get the best out of land banking. Whenever people chat me up saying they want to invest in land banking, I first ask, "What's your budget?" I have more than 20 estates, and I cannot tell you about each of them one by one; that would be a waste of both our time. Telling me your budget would help me give you the properties close to your budget. The second question I would ask is, "What location do you want?" That is because I sell properties in Nigeria, Dubai, the U.K, and the U.S.

Most times, these budgets are not enough for the property you want to buy; hence, you have to raise it. You are not ready to invest in real estate if you don't want to raise your budget. Don't say you don't have enough; you have something to start, put it together.

"Always know that the ultimate desire of God for your life is that you can do the impossible with the available."

You will never have it all. I don't have it all, either. People see me on social media and think I have all the money in the world. I do not have it all. As I write this book, I am looking for 20 billion dollars. I constantly look for money to keep developing my estates by building houses, fencing them, and providing infrastructure because it's so much work to build an estate. You have to start by looking for money to pay for the land; then you move to look for money to develop the land, and then you move to look for money to build the house itself. It requires much money, so you constantly need money, and will never have enough. So, have a budget, start investing with it, and raise it as time goes on.

FOOD FOR THOUGHT

- *"Human beings cannot help you keep the kind of money they've never handled before."*

- *"People cannot be faithful in helping you manage your resources which they have never managed for themselves."*

- *"Anybody going to design a cloth for you, check the designers he or she is wearing."*

If somebody is going to teach you how to manage your resources, wealth, and funds, research who they are and how they have managed their own because they ultimately cannot give you what they do not have. In a nutshell, get a mentor that has results.

PART SIX
STRATEGIC INVESTMENT LOCATIONS

CHAPTER 19
100% Return On Investment On Land Banking At Sapphire Estate, Ikorodu

Ikorodu is the next big thing that will happen to Lagos after Ibeju-Lekki. It is a bubble land, and bubble lands experience high developmental rates. Ibeju-Lekki is far more expensive than Ikorodu, yet, people are starting to live in Ibeju-Lekki like Ikorodu. The population in Ikorodu is more significant compared to that of Ibeju-Lekki. More people are migrating there now. This astonishing fact is unique, and you can take advantage of it.

An example is one of our estates in Owutu, Mile 12 area, just before one enters Ikorodu town. Those areas are densely populated with people living in those locations; however, places in Ibeju-Lekki worth ten to fifteen million naira are yet to have people living in those areas like this. As such, they may have good titles but lack population growth. Because of this, you might not be able to live there upon purchase. But for Ikorodu, you can start building once you purchase the land, move in, and even meet more than enough people to exchange pleasantries within just 2 minute's walk from your land. The place where our estate, Sapphire Water City, is situated is even far more developed than the significant parts of Ikorodu. It's closer to Mile 12 Market, before the main Ikorodu town, with fast access to the Airport, Berger, Victoria Island etc. One unique thing about Sapphire Estate is that it is in a central location.

One of our credibility is sharing videos with you even after you have sent family members to inspect the land for you, because some give you wrong or inadequate information upon return. These are more reasons why I engage in live Facebook videos most of the time.

Around Sapphire estate, people already live on this axis as there's electricity, and it's pretty habitable. Thus, there's nothing wrong with you building your house in an area where in less than 2 minute's walk; you have more than enough people to interact with.

However, the only disadvantage people attribute Ikorodu with is that it has much water. But then, I have often emphasised how water is always better and never a disadvantage when it comes to investment, particularly land banking. That is because, in many cases, when it comes to land banking, you are not buying because you want to live in the house; you're buying so that you can resell at a higher price later in the future. You're buying to own and not to use.

These are some of the land banking secrets, and secret means that most people don't know; else, they would've taken advantage of it. The beautiful thing about these secrets is that if you take advantage of them, you ultimately have benefits for yourself. Before you ask, 'What do you mean by the benefits to yourself?' I'm still going to recap but let's proceed.

Lands in Benin do not appreciate much because—I taught you these secrets—you do not invest in land banking based on sentiments, i.e., where I am from. So, don't buy land in your village yet. Here's the reason. If I buy land in my village, it will not appreciate like the one in Lagos. So, the concept of land banking is that you're buying land that will appreciate in the long run.

CHAPTER 20
Conclusion

I want you always to remember this: **Land Banking** is the future. So when you invest in landed properties, be sure that you will get a 100% return on investment.

If you leave your money in the bank, trust me, you will get little or no return on investment (ROI), but if you invest wisely into land banking, be assured that you will get a hundred percent ROI. Therefore, I employ you not to relent, take advantage of the opportunities presented in this book and own a landed property with Gtext Homes.

One of the big mistakes people make when doing land banking is that they tell too many people, and end up getting discouraged from buying; instead, they will advise them to buy a car.

And my question to them is, "Are you trying to impress people that really don't care, or are you consciously making this investment because you know it will change your life once you get the 100% return on investment in a few years?"

Imagine someone that used their last savings to buy a car in the 1980s. You know the car must have been outdated by now. The same money they used to buy the car if they were to have bought a house or land in the 1980s, imagine the value of the house or land now. You must have been a multi-billionaire by now; the whole world would have celebrated your wealth.

Don't rush to buy a car model because everyone is getting it, to receive accolades; instead, buy land and watch it appreciate in 10 to 20 years' time, and people will begin to envy you and admire you.

In Africa, people always make you feel guilty for investing your money wisely while everybody is doing parties and buying cars around you. But, if you start investing in properties or buying land on days you are not financially stable, and you will see family members and everybody on your neck.

Poor people spend all their money buying luxurious items, the latest hair, clothes, bags or shoes, but the wise always use their sayings to invest in real estate. They do everything they can to secure their financial future.

There are lands we bought at 4.5 million naira and sold at 20 million naira a few years later. Is this not 100% profit? Yeah, it's not everybody whose source of wealth is questionable. If you start doing land banking correctly, you will become a billionaire in less than 10 years.

If you're a woman reading this book, you must be your husband's investment partner. My wife has been so supportive. She's a wise woman. So ladies, instead of telling your husband you need bone straight and all, tell them to buy a landed property first. Then, when it appreciates, there will be more money to buy anything you want. I'm not saying that, as a woman, you cannot go into the real estate business yourself; you can. I have seen many women succeed in the real estate industry. I am saying that you need to be visionary and delay gratification.

Encourage your husband to invest in real estate. That's a way of securing your generation's future because, in land banking, there is always a 100% return on investment.

Remember, land banking is not an overnight success story. You don't start from the top; instead, you start from the bottom and get to the top. Everything great in life starts from the bottom, then gradually, grows over time, and you keep finding the opportunity to expand.

Invest in land banking, get your proper documents, and build wealth. At Gtext Homes, we ensure we send the complete documents to anyone who bought our landed properties, no matter any part of the world they live in. The documents include the Deed of Assignment and Survey, and we have partnered with

DHL and UPS for worldwide delivery.

I have had people who said they have family members in Nigeria who can help them pick it up. Our answer is usually no because we don't want stories. Even if you want your family member to be here physically when you're buying the land, we do a virtual streaming where you can see the land or property you're buying virtually. So it's like a virtual tour of the land or property you're buying.

Suppose you want to buy any property, contact, Gtext Homes. It's not something that you should be scared of. As I mentioned earlier, even if you invest now in five to ten years, you can sell and have your 100% return on investment.

Remember, "you don't wait to buy land; you buy land and wait!"

See you at the top!

GTEXT HOMES PROPERTIES AND LOCATIONS

Prime Rose Farm City, Itamarun, Ibeju-Lekki, Lagos State

Sapphire Water City, Isawo-Owutu, Ikorodu, Lagos State

Jasper Estate, Lugbe, Abuja

BECOMING A BILLIONAIRE LAND BANKER

Beryl Golf Estate, Lagos-Ibadan Expressway, Ibadan

Jasper Beach and Golf Estate, Ibeju-Lekki, Lagos State

White House Estate, Atan, Ogun State

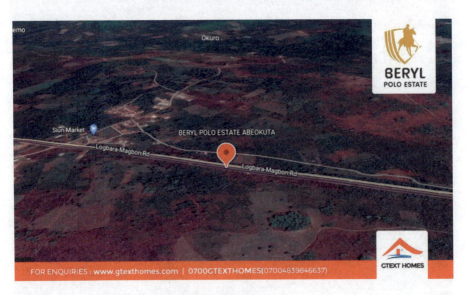

Beryl Polo Estate, Abeokuta, Ogun State

Beryl Beach Front, Idado-Elecko, Ibeju-Lekki, Lagos State

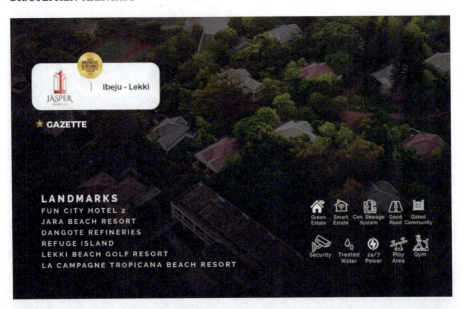

BECOMING A BILLIONAIRE LAND BANKER

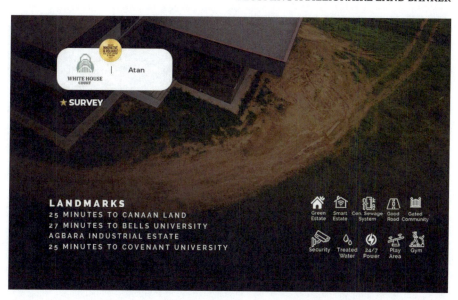

BECOMING A BILLIONAIRE LAND BANKER

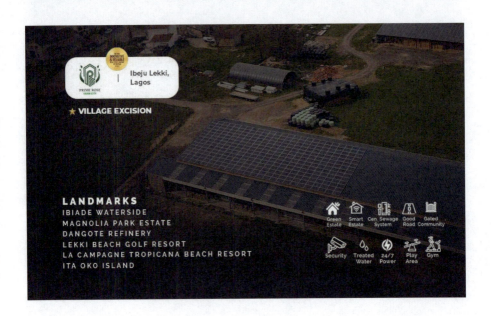

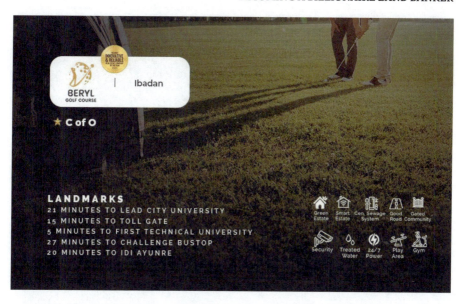

BERYL GOLF COURSE | Ibadan

★ C of O

LANDMARKS
21 MINUTES TO LEAD CITY UNIVERSITY
15 MINUTES TO TOLL GATE
5 MINUTES TO FIRST TECHNICAL UNIVERSITY
27 MINUTES TO CHALLENGE BUSTOP
20 MINUTES TO IDI AYUNRE

Green Estate | Smart Estate | Cen. Sewage System | Good Road | Gated Community
Security | Treated Water | 24/7 Power | Play Area | Gym

Sardius CREEK | Ogudu, Lagos

★ C of O

LANDMARKS
- OGUDU GRA.
- ABIOLA GARDEN.
- OGUDU MALL.
- GANI FAWEHINMI FREEDOM PARK.
- PRAISEVILLE GARDEN ESTATE PHASE 1.
- THE PLACE RESTAURANT.
- NORMADIC NEGRO.
- OPPOSITE THIRD MAINLAND BRIDGE

Green Estate | Smart Estate | Cen. Sewage System | Good Road | Gated Community
Security | Treated Water | 24/7 Power | Play Area | Gym

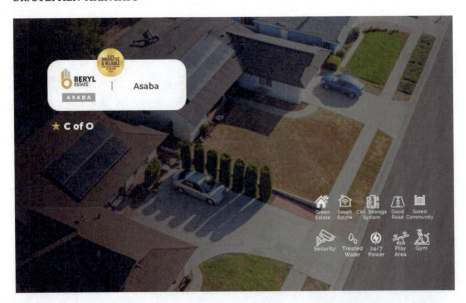

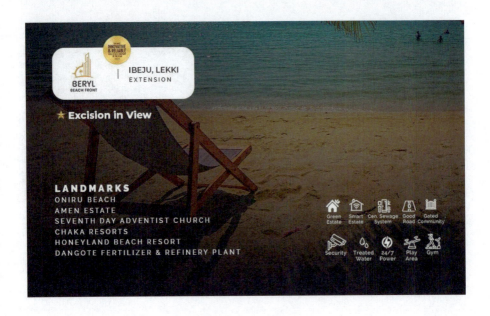

BECOMING A BILLIONAIRE LAND BANKER

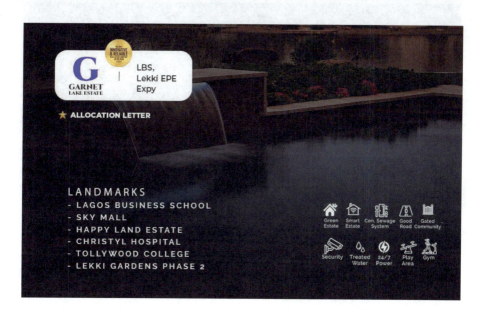

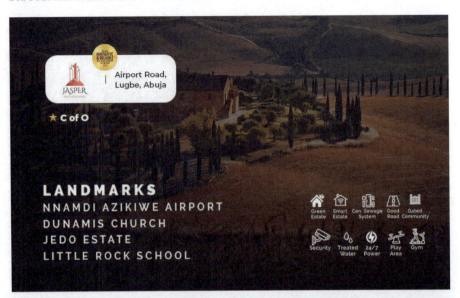

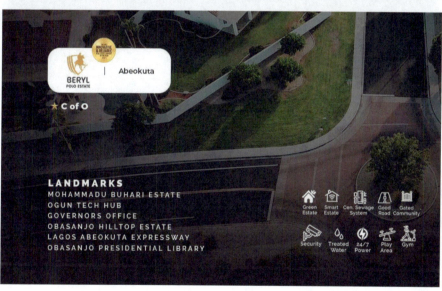

ABOUT THE AUTHOR

Dr. Stephen Akintayo

He is Africa's most influential Investment Coach. He is a member of the Forbes Business Council, an invitation-only organisation for successful entrepreneurs and business leaders worldwide.

He is a Serial Entrepreneur and the GMD/CEO of Gtext Holdings, the mother company of different subsidiaries, including Gtext Homes, a Real Estate company with a highly innovative and young workforce, owning over 20 estates. It is based in Nigeria, with Headquarters in Banana Island, Lagos, Nigeria, and other branches including Omole Phase 1, Lagos; Abuja, FCT; Ibadan, Oyo State; Abeokuta, Ogun State; Asaba, Delta state, and Port Harcourt, Rivers State, all in Nigeria. Gtext Homes also has offices in Dubai, United Arab Emirates (UAE); London, United Kingdom and a proposed office in Dallas, USA. She has a workforce of over 300 people.

Other subsidiaries include Stephen Akintayo Consulting (SAC), its Headquarters in Dubai, UAE. It is poised to raise entrepreneurs who will lead the world of business and investments in Nigeria, Africa, and the world. It raises these entrepreneurs through mentorship, practical and in-depth training in courses such as; Real Estate brokerage and investment, E-commerce, Digital marketing, Cryptocurrency, Forex Trading, Stocks and Shares, Business Structure and Grants, Talent Monetization etc.

Stephen Akintayo Consulting has a vision of raising 1 million millionaires by the year 2050, with 70% of them from African heritage and others who are Africans in the diaspora. That led to the creation of Stephen Akintayo Online Wealth University in 2020.

The Stephen Akintayo Wealth University is an Online Wealth Creation School. This university was formed after realising that formal education doesn't teach about money and wealth creation. Hence, a university that does that was created for people to study and get certified upon completion. This university aims to broaden the knowledge base and further sharpen the skills of young people with our numerous practical and time-tested courses.

Another outstanding subsidiary is Ginido (an E-commerce platform), formerly Gilead Balm. It has hundreds of organisations as its clients, including multinational companies like Heritage Bank, Guarantee Trust Bank, P.Z. Cussons, MTN, Chivita, DHL, and GNLD, amongst others. Gtext Global has also diversified into the agricultural sector with the subsidiary Gtext Farms. Gtext Farms has a substantial equity investment in Allanisaqriq Limited, which started in 2012. It is focused on cash crop exportation, with a warehouse at Kano, Kogi, Abuja, and over 100 acres of Cashew farm in Oyo State, Nigeria. Gtext Farms plans to grow into Nigeria's largest Cashew crop processor and organic farm by 2035. Subsequently, other subsidiaries like Gtext Land, Gtext Academy, Gtext Hub, Gtext and Associates, Guest, and Gtext Soft have been formed and have also birthed massive results.

The Founder of Gtext Holdings, formerly known as Gilead Balm Group Services, has assisted several businesses in Nigeria to move to enviable levels by aiding them reach their clients through its enormous nationwide database of actual phone numbers and email addresses. It has hundreds of organisations as its clients, including multinational companies.

He was born in the Gonge area of Maiduguri, Borno State, the

North Eastern part of Nigeria, in a very impoverished environment with a civil servant mother who raised him and his four other siblings with her meagre salary. His father's contract business had crumbled before he was born. His upbringing informed his passion for philanthropy. In his words, ". Hunger was my biggest challenge. I had to scavenge all through primary school to eat lunch, as I didn't go to school with lunch packs. We were too poor to afford that, but things got better in my secondary school days. Although, my mum would go to her colleagues to borrow money to send me to school each term. Seeing them looking at my mum with utter dismay as someone who keeps begging was humiliating. It hurt dearly. I hated poverty and prayed to help more families.

Dr Stephen learned to spell the word "THE" in JSS 1. However, his educational background was faulty. You could easily conclude that Stephen will never amount to anything in life. He spent ages 8-12 in an environment without electricity, within a forest region of Maiduguri-Damboa road. "I laid on a mattress at age 13 for the first time", he said.

At 17, he read his first business book, "Rich Dad, Poor Dad" and the rest is history today. He started a business at the age of 17, selling food supplements by GNLD, introduced to him by his cousin. And his first online-based business was selling E-books he bought for N3,000. He ventured into other businesses in the process. However, his main drive to succeed was to compensate a very hardworking mother who denied herself everything to educate her 5 children. While a student, he organised students' trade fairs within the students' community. It was during his higher education that his mother died of Ovarian Cancer at the age of 24. That was the most challenging season of his life and business career, as his mother had been his leading financier. If there was anyone who believed in his entrepreneurial skill, it was his mother. One of his staff once said he was not a businessman because of his soft-outspokenness and willingness to share his success secrets with others–qualities he learned from his mother.

"The day you start giving is the day you start living. The day you stop giving is the day you start dying. Give daily to live daily. Give joy, counsel, give smiles, give food and give creative business ideas, to change the world" - Stephen Akintayo. Dr Stephen Akintayo's story is true of grass to grace. His only regret is that his hardworking mother died a few years before he got the big break, not witnessing what she had always wished for.

In 2020, Dr Stephen Akintayo took giant strides that landed the entire conglomerate on the global scene, expanding business networks to 4 continents of the world. As a result, the business empire has grown to a multi-billion naira corporation, with the vision to take over the centre stage in the Real Estate and Digital Marketing sectors.

He is also the Founder and President of the Stephen Akintayo Foundation, formerly called Infinity Foundation. Infinity Foundation started in 2008 as a student Non- Governmental Organization (NGO) with a group of 13 students who donated N3,000 each to impact an orphanage in Ibadan, Western Nigeria, called Galilee Foundation.

The Stephen Akintayo Foundation has aided orphans and vulnerable children and has mentored young minds. The Foundation has assisted over 2,000 orphans and vulnerable children. It has also partnered with over 25 orphanage homes in the country. The Foundation has also cared for victims of Boko Haram attacks in the North-Eastern part of Nigeria. The Stephen Akintayo Foundation focuses on donating relief materials, food and financial grants for school children and entrepreneurs. It offered grants of 10,000,000 Naira to 20 entrepreneurs in 2015, grants of $1,000 for the Instagram business challenge in 2021, and 500,000 Naira each to 4 winners of the Billionaire Habits book challenge in 2021.

In January and February 2022, the Foundation gave a total of 10 million Naira as a bursary to less privileged students of the nursery, primary, and secondary schools to aid their learning.

From 2023 - 2027, the Foundation plans to empower over 500 entrepreneurs with a grant of $5,000 each across different sectors, technology and United Nations Sustainable Development Goal (UNSDGs) driven. At the end of the 5 years, the Stephen Akintayo Foundation would have given $5 million to African entrepreneurs.

He is a prolific author who has 41 books to his name. The best-selling Billionaire Habits book, and the sequel, the Billionaire Codes, have sold thousands of copies globally, with book reviews in over 50 cities, building habits of billionaires in people. Other books include; Survival Instincts, The Information Millionaire, Maximising your Real Estate Investment, and Managing Family Finance, amongst other life-transforming books.

Dr Stephen is a media personality in the Television, Radio, and Print media. He ran a series on the radio, tagged: CEO Mentorship with Stephen Akintayo. In 2020, he started the revolutionary business TV Show: Investment Chat in a Rolls Royce with Dr Stephen Akintayo, a perfect blend of luxury, entertainment, and investment talks. The T.V. show is two-phased, the Nigerian and Dubai series. The Nigerian series has been airing since 2020 on Channels Television and his social media platforms–Facebook and YouTube.

In 2021, he took the show to Dubai and how much of a huge success it was! He also started the Learning Luxury Show in Dubai and is on the 3rd edition of the show. He has also started his podcast called The Billionaire Habits Podcast, which is aimed at bringing successful entrepreneurs on the platform who had a poor beginning and have made it legitimately to inspire and educate young people. The first edition was shot and produced in Dubai, UAE.

In February 2022, he started the shooting of his 3rd show, Big Talk with DSA–a political show aimed at resetting the minds of youths and empowering them with the proper knowledge to birth a new nation. In 2021, he also hosted the Global Property Brokers Conference, the largest Brokers Conference in Africa. It is now renamed to the Global Property Festival with international business moguls such as Grant Cardone, Ryan Serhant, and the number one coach in the world, John C. Maxwell, as co-speakers.

In 2022, he organised the Global Wealth Festival in 3 locations worldwide–Nigeria, London, and the United States of America. The first location of the festival was in Dallas, which was held in July 2022, featuring Grant Cardone as the Keynote speaker. He also hosted the Global Leadership Conference in Dubai, with Ex-president Olusegun Obasanjo as the Keynote speaker. He has also hosted Robert Kiyosaki, Dr Brian Tracy, and Dr Les Brown on the Billionaire Habits Masterclass webinar–a global webinar to instil the habits of successful billionaires into young people and how they can replicate the same.

He's also the convener of the Believers' Wealth Conference and the Family Finance Conference, which teach the believers of the Gospel of Christ and couples how to build legitimate transgenerational wealth for themselves. He hosts a yearly conference called the Upgrade Summit, held at the beginning of every year to prepare young people worldwide for the coming year and how they can achieve giant strides. His mentorship platform has a broad reach as it caters to personal and corporate development. Dr Stephen strongly believes young Nigerians with a passion for entrepreneurship can cause a business revolution in Nigeria and the world. Little wonder why his business empire is run by young, fly, and rich folks.

His first degree was in Microbiology from Olabisi Onabanjo University, Ogun state, Nigeria. He is a member of the Institute of Strategic Management (ISMN). He also graduated from the Harvard University Executive program, where he studied Essential Management Skills for Emerging Leaders and Real Estate Investment.

In 2020, he was awarded a Doctor of Science, D.Sc (Honoris Causa) in Real Estate Development and Corporate Leadership by the European American University. He is also a trained coach by the Coaching Academy, U.K.

He is a multiple award winner happily married and blessed with three children; two fabulous boys and a lovely girl.

To invite Dr Stephen Akintayo for a speaking engagement, kindly visit www.stephenakintayo.com/booking or email ea@stephenakintayo.com. You can also reach him via +2348180000618 or +971 58 828 3572.

OTHER BOOKS BY THE SAME AUTHOR

1. Billionaire Habits
2. Billionaire Codes
3. Maximising your real estate investment
4. Start a business from ground up
5. How to earn 6 figures from digital marketing
6. Mental wealth
7. Managing family finance
8. Entrepreneurial Tools
9. Millionaire freelancer
10. The good, bad and ugly of investing in Africa
11. The story behind the glory
12. Survival instincts
13. Business Mentorship
14. Becoming a sales machine
15. Advanced mini-importation
16. Speaking and writing
17. Billionaire investor
18. Cryptocurrency leverage
19. Information Millionaire
20. The online money book

21. Building wealthy relationships

22. Farming is the new oil

23. Visa made easy

24. Millionaire blogger

25. Scholarship made easy

26. Mobile Millionaire

27. Weight loss

28. Locate

29. The law of poverty and wealth

30. Fastest ways to make money through affiliate marketing

31. How to make fast money from social media marketing

32. Becoming a freelance guru

33. Corporate marketing with email campaigns

34. Digital Marketer

35. Affiliate business cash flow

36. Switch

37. Turn your mess to your message

38. Mobile Millionaire 2

39. Billionaire Habits for Pastors

40. Billionaire Habits for Entrepreneurs

You can get any of these books on Amazon or Stephen Akintayo Store, https://store.stephenakintayo.com, or contact +971 58 828 3572 or +234 818 0000 618, or send an email to products@stephenakintayo.com.

GTEXT HOMES OFFICES AROUND THE WORLD

1. Headquarters, Lagos Island: Banana Island, Lagos State.
2. Lagos Mainland: 25A Lola Holloway, Omole Phase 1, Lagos State.
3. Ibadan: 15, Unity Road, Yellow Gate, Oluyole Extension, Ibadan.
4. Abuja: 1314b, Wikki Springs Street, IBB Boulevard, Maitama, Abuja.
5. Port Harcourt: 3B Road 21, 1st Avenue, NAF Harmony Estate, Port Harcourt.
6. Abeokuta: Nō 6, Tunde Osokoya street, off Keem Hotel Road, Ibara GRA, Abeokuta.
7. Dubai: Gtext Hub, 2404 Al Moosa Tower 2, Sheikh Zayed Road, Dubai.
8. U.K: 133 Wennington Road, Upminster, Havering, United Kingdom, RM13 9TR.

You can visit us if you are in any of these locations, or call the number +2348188111999 for directions. We would be glad to receive you.

CONNECT WITH DR. STEPHEN AKINTAYO ON THESE SOCIAL MEDIA PLATFORMS

Twitter - http://www.stephenakintayo.com/twitter

Tiktok - http://www.stephenakintayo.com/tiktok

Facebook - http://www.stephenakintayo.com/facebook

Instagram - http://www.stephenakintayo.com/instagram

YouTube - http://www.stephenakintayo.com/youtube

LinkedIn - http://www.stephenakintayo.com/linkedin

Email - stephenakintayo@gmail.com

Made in the USA
Columbia, SC
03 June 2024